SO TO THE LAND

So to the land our hearts we give
   Till the sure magic strike,
And Memory, Use, and Love make live
   Us and our fields alike –
That deeper than our speech and thought,
   Beyond our reason's sway,
Clay of the pit whence we were wrought
   Yearns to its fellow-clay.

from *Sussex*
Rudyard Kipling

To Carl

SO TO THE LAND

An Anthology of
Countryside Poetry

Selected and introduced
by
DIANA RIGG

Wood Engravings by
Christopher Wormell

HEADLINE

First published in 1994
by HEADLINE BOOK PUBLISHING

10 9 8 7 6 5 4 3 2 1

British Library Cataloguing in Publication Data

So to the Land ...: Anthology of
countryside poetry
I. Rigg, Diana
821.0080321734

ISBN 0 7472 1019 5

Typeset by
Letterpart Limited, Reigate, Surrey

Printed and bound in Great Britain by
Mackays of Chatham PLC, Chatham, Kent

HEADLINE BOOK PUBLISHING
A division of Hodder Headline PLC
338 Euston Road
London NW1 3BH

ACKNOWLEDGEMENTS

The many friends who suggested sources.

Maggie and Kate, who gallantly typed out poems and pretended they enjoyed it.

Last, but not least, Sylvia Greenwood, who introduced me, as an eleven-year-old, to poetry and had that rare gift, as a teacher, to engender a lasting love for it.

For permission to reprint copyright material the editor and the publishers gratefully acknowledge the following:

Secker & Warburg and the Peters Fraser & Dunlop Group Ltd for 'The Buzzards' from *Collected Poems* by Martin Armstrong; Faber & Faber Ltd for 'On This Island' from *Collected Poems* by W.H. Auden; Pimlico (a division of Random Century) and the Peters Fraser & Dunlop Group Ltd for 'Sonnet IV' and 'Sonnet XXV' from *Complete Verse* by Hilaire Belloc; John Murray (Publishers) Ltd for 'Winter Seascape' from *Collected Poems* by John Betjeman; Sidgwick & Jackson and the Peters Fraser & Dunlop Group Ltd for 'The Pike' from *The Waggoner and Other Poems*, and Carcanet Press Ltd for 'Winter: East Anglia' from *Selected Poems* (1982), by Edmund Blunden; Seren Books for 'Wild Duck' by Euros Bowen, from *Welsh Verse*, tr. Tony Conran; the Earl of Strathmore and Kinghorne for 'The White Hare' from *Collected Poems* by Lilian Bowes Lyon; Macmillan London Ltd for 'Squirrel' by John Buxton; John Johnson (Authors' Agent) Ltd for 'A Frosty Night' from *Turning Point* by Philip Callow; Macmillan London Ltd and David Higham Associates Ltd for 'Tam Snow' and 'At Candlemas' from *Collected Poems* by Charles Causley; Macmillan Publishing Company for 'Now is the Time' from *Summer Green* by Elizabeth Coatsworth, Copyright © 1940 by Macmillan Publishing Company, renewed 1968 by Elizabeth Coatsworth Beston; Seren Books for Tony Conran's translations of 'Heather' by Eifion Wyn, 'Hunting the Hare', and 'Winter', in *Welsh Verse*; Sinclair-Stevenson Ltd for 'Harebells over Mannin Bay', 'Windy Day in August', 'A Hard Frost' and 'The Fox' from *The Complete Poems* (1992) by C. Day Lewis; the Literary Trustees of Walter de la Mare, and the Society of Authors as their representative, for 'The Willow', 'The Moth', 'The Scarecrow' and 'The Rainbow' from *The Complete Poems of Walter de la Mare* (1969); Faber & Faber Ltd for 'Rannoch, by Glencoe' from *Collected Poems 1909-1962* by T.S. Eliot; the author and Poet and Printer (Alan Tarling) for 'May' from *The Aerial Noctiluca* by Peter Forbes; Faber & Faber Ltd for 'Considering the Snail' from *Collected Poems* by Thom Gunn; P. Harvey, and Douglas McLean at the Forest Bookshop, for 'November' from the *Collected Poems* by F.W. Harvey; Faber & Faber Ltd for 'Trout', 'Blackberry-Picking' and 'Waterfall' from *Death of a Naturalist* by Seamus

CONTENTS

DEDICATION

___

To Chips and Sarah

FOREWORD

I am not a countrywoman, for I wasn't born in the country; more to the point, I spent the first seven years of my life in India. Just before Independence my brother and I were brought back to England and put into boarding schools, while our mother returned to India. Nowadays such a split in the family would be considered damaging, but over forty years ago it was the 'done thing' and thought to be in our best interests.

My school, in Buckinghamshire, was a strange place. Most of the children had been similarly dispossessed of their parents, and the Headmistress more or less left us alone to run wild. There were lessons, of course, but in retrospect we seemed to spend most of our waking hours in the very large garden behind the house. The trees, predominantly tall old pines, became the focus of our lives. We each bagged one as our own, fearlessly climbed up them like monkeys, and, as high as we dared, we built nests, criss-crossing sticks and interweaving these with fronds of fir. To this day I find the smell of pine, and the sound of the wind in the trees, deeply comforting.

It was from the top of my tree that I distinctly remember seeing, for the first time, a panoramic view of the countryside around. Golden fields sectioned by dark hedges, a village, a spire, clumps of tall trees and, on the skyline, a rise of hills that were always slightly misty. I used to pray to whatever, whoever, lay beyond those hills, to go back to India, to make it up with my best friends, never to be made to eat porridge again – we were served it for breakfast winter and summer – but most fervently, for the French Mistress to be struck by lightning.

My parents returned in 1947 and the family moved to a city in Yorkshire, where our customary Sunday afternoon drives did little to broaden my scant experience of the countryside. I used to sit in the back of the car, cocooned and dreaming, while the Dales slid past the windows, much like back projection in a film studio.

Picnics were taken in the corners of fields, close to the road, and walks restricted to well-worn paths. Land, I learnt, was owned by other people, and we weren't to trespass upon it. Once, on holiday in Devon, I witnessed a hunt when the stag swam out to sea, exactly as described in 'A Runnable Stag' by John Davidson (page 87). For months afterwards I dreamt about it, reliving the feelings of helplessness and grief as I watched the stag's head cut through the sea, never once turning back.

By now I had discovered poetry and the power it held to transport me anywhere, at any time, beyond the restrictions of my life. When I was eleven I was given a copy of W.H. Davies' *Collected Poems*, and it was he who first inspired my journey. Keats, Wordsworth and Browning followed, and from then on, there was no stopping me. My view of nature, of course, was wholly romantic and it wasn't until 1962, when I took a cottage on the outskirts of a village in Warwickshire, that I began to make any connection between the image on the page and what I could see for myself. The cottage was Elizabethan, long, low and scarcely modernized. It even had an outside lavatory, an arrangement which, if you have never experienced it, I can highly recommend. From my throne, the view across the fields was lovely, particularly in the early morning. A pair of swallows nested under the roof and became very cross each time I dared to enter their domain.

At one end of my cottage was a separate dwelling, where Arthur lived. He must have been in his nineties, and was very stooped, toothless and garrulous. Gradually we got to know one another, and through the summer I spent many contented hours sitting in his garden, dwarfed by the huge, flamboyant dahlias he loved to grow, while he told me about his life.

His accounts of his early years were particularly fascinating, since they gave me an insight into a previous century and very much tougher times. Arthur's family were poor farm-labouring stock, and as a very young boy he had gone to Stratford-upon-Avon's Mop Fair and stood in a pen, as was customary in those days, with other farm labourers, waiting to be hired. His first employer turned out to be a particularly cruel taskmaster. He worked the boy all hours and even on Sundays, the only day off, insisted that Arthur attend church, which meant a walk of several miles. 'I was so tired I used to fall asleep in the hedgerow on my way back,' he said. Luckily Arthur knew about the Runaway Fair, held some weeks after the Mop for people who, like him, were unhappy in their hirings. So he plucked up his courage, stole away, and this time ended up happily working on another farm until he retired.

As we talked, he would draw my attention to a tree, a bird, an insect, and with each identification would come some nugget of country lore. There was nothing, it seemed to me, that he didn't know about nature or the land. My admiration for him was unbounded, but patently not reciprocated, for Arthur considered my lifestyle and concerns to be utterly worthless, and said as much. Working the land all his life, he knew it as well as he knew his own body, and accompanying this knowledge was a respect and a deep, almost possessive love.

Not long after our encounters began, I decided to explore the surrounding countryside for myself. With no sense of direction, I simply followed my instincts and roamed for miles around. Gradually, I shed the city dweller's fear of getting lost or being shouted at for trespassing. Whenever I became tired I sat and rested, at the edge of a field or in a wood, and watched and listened. Increasingly I began to experience the separate senses of sight, sound, touch and smell that such solitude engenders. I noticed when the wind changed direction, the details on the bark of a tree picked out by the sunlight, the distant thrumming of a woodpecker. It was fascinating. By the time the summer had ended and I had packed my bags and said goodbye to Arthur, I knew, as I drove away, that this new-found delight would remain with me for the rest of my life.

Compiling this book has given me many happy hours in the countryside, albeit second hand. I first thought of putting together such a collection some time ago. For years I have been invited by a friend to fish trout on a particularly glorious stretch of the Test. Now, only those who are passionate about fishing would understand the pleasure I have received, and the burden of my debt. When I asked what I could possibly present by way of recompense, my friend said, 'A book of country poetry.'

This was a simple enough request, I thought, and I began the search to fulfil it. I looked in bookshop after bookshop, but nowhere could I find exactly what I sensed was wanted. After a time I became desperate, for there appeared to be no other solution than to set about compiling a book myself. So I did.

I have tried to put together something along the lines of a poetic diary of the countryside, taking the reader on a simultaneous journey – through the course of a day in each season, and through the season itself. I have included the birds, animals, trees, flowers and insects associated with the season, and also the sporting pursuits, fishing necessarily being one. In order to achieve my aim, the poet had to possess a naturalist's eye, and to practise simplicity. The Elizabethans, for example, favoured the device of taking aspects of nature to illustrate the human condition, and though often charming, this seemed too artificial for my purposes. The Romantics, of course, saw the countryside through a soft-focus lens, while the Augustans draped everything in classical allusions, to the point where nature becomes hardly recognisable, still less native. The 'I' of the poet seemed similarly intrusive. Not to say that exceptions to these reservations won't be found in the book, for some poems are too good to omit.

Down the years, of course, many of the same themes and observations are repeated, such as cuckoos and daffodils in spring, or frost and snow in winter. Besides these, however, I have attempted to vary the calendar to include the unexpected and arresting. For I love poetry and never more than when a poet's art flushes my imagination from its accustomed torpor.

Lastly – there exist grander vistas, brighter colours and far more exotic manifestations of nature elsewhere, but I believe our countryside to be unparalleled, and many of those who wrote about it, matchless. Of course I am biased; yet, what began in answer to a simple request, I hope also does homage in small measure to this land and its poets.

Diana

June, 1994

SPRING

And now all Nature seem'd in love;
The lusty sap began to move;
New juice did stir th'embracing vines;
And birds had drawn their valentines.
The jealous trout, that low did lie,
Rose at a well-dissembled flie:

. . . .

The showers were short, the weather mild,
The morning fresh, the evening smil'd.

from On a Bank as I Sat Fishing,
in *Reliquiae Wottonianae*
Sir Henry Wotton

from CRAVING FOR SPRING

by D.H. Lawrence

I wish it were spring in the world.

Let it be spring!
Come, bubbling, surging tide of sap!
Come, rush of creation!
Come, life! surge through this mass of mortification!
Come, sweep away these exquisite, ghastly first-flowers,
    which are rather last-flowers!
Come, thaw down their cool portentousness, dissolve
    them;
snowdrops, straight, death-veined exhalations of white
    and purple crocuses,
flowers of the penumbra, issue of corruption, nourished in
    mortification,
jets of exquisite finality;
Come, spring, make havoc of them!

I trample on the snowdrops, it gives me pleasure to tread
    down the jonquils,
to destroy the chill Lent lilies;
for I am sick of them, their faint-bloodedness,
slow-blooded, icy-fleshed, portentous.

I want the fine, kindly wine-sap of spring,
gold, and of inconceivably fine, quintessential brightness,
rare almost as beams, yet overwhelmingly potent,
strong like the greatest force of world-balancing.

This is the same that picks up the harvest of wheat
and rocks it, tons of grain, on the ripening wind;
the same that dangles the globe-shaped pleiads of fruit
temptingly in mid-air, between a playful thumb and
    finger;
oh, and suddenly, from out of nowhere, whirls the
    pear-bloom,
upon us, and apple- and almond- and apricot- and
    quince-blossom,
storms and cumulus clouds of all imaginable blossom
about our bewildered faces,
though we do not worship.

I wish it were spring
cunningly blowing on the fallen sparks, odds and ends of
    the old, scattered fire,
and kindling shapely little conflagrations
curious long-legged foals, and wide-eared calves, and
    naked sparrow-bubs.

I wish that spring
would start the thundering traffic of feet
new feet on the earth, beating with impatience.

A Schule Laddie's Lament on the Lateness o' the Season

by James Logie Robertson

The east wind's whistlin' cauld an' shrill,
The snaw lies on the Lomont Hill;
It's simmer i' the almanack,
But when 'ill simmer days be back?

There's no' a bud on tree or buss;
The craws are at a sair nonplus, –
Hoo can they big? hoo can they pair?
Wi' them sae cauld, and winds sae bare.

My faither canna saw his seed, –
The hauf o' th' laund's to ploo, indeed;
The lambs are deein', an' the yowes
Are trauchled wanderin' owre the knowes.

Ther's no' a swallow back as yet,
The robin doesna seek to flit;
There's no' a buckie, nor a bud,
On ony brae, in ony wud.

It's no' a time for barefit feet
When it may be on-ding o' sleet.
The season's broken a' oor rules, –
It's no' the time o' year o' bools;

It's no' the time o' year o' peeries.
I think the year's gane tapsalteeries!
The farmers may be bad, nae doot –
It pits hiz laddies sair aboot.

CYCLAMENS

by 'Michael Field'
(Katharine Bradley and Edith Cooper)

They are terribly white:
There is snow on the ground,
  And a moon on the snow at night;
  The sky is cut by the winter light;
Yet I, who have all these things in ken,
Am struck to the heart by the chiselled white
  Of this handful of cyclamen.

FIRST SIGHT

by Philip Larkin

Lambs that learn to walk in snow
When their bleating clouds the air
Meet a vast unwelcome, know
Nothing but a sunless glare.
Newly stumbling to and fro
All they find, outside the fold,
Is a wretched width of cold.

As they wait beside the ewe,
Her fleeces wetly caked, there lies
Hidden round them, waiting too,
Earth's immeasurable surprise.
They could not grasp it if they knew,
What so soon will wake and grow
Utterly unlike the snow.

LAST SNOW

by Andrew Young

Although the snow still lingers
Heaped on the ivy's blunt webbed fingers
And painted tree-trunks on one side,
Here in this sunlit ride
The fresh unchristened things appear,
Leaf, spathe and stem,
With crumbs of earth clinging to them
To show the way they came
But no flower yet to tell their name,
And one green spear
Stabbing a dead leaf from below
Kills winter at a blow.

Snowdrops

by Christopher D. Panton

As damp perfume rises from winter's ground,
The elements combine to make living inhospitable.
Pushing, elbowing, cream yellow points
Thrust upward, toward the light,
Enter the air from beneath to turn green.

Live shoots, tiny, fragile encroached by
Boulders, pit heap mounds, a lunar landscape;
Crushable to a child's hand, they withstand the exposure
Of brittle white mornings with frigid wind,
When soil becomes stone,
And metalled water stops its flow.

White star hung bells, edged with green,
Defy winter's tantrums;
Brave scouts of spring that shrug off
Cold discomfort, unconscious of desolate environment,
They see only their own beauty clustered there;
Each one in love with another,
Nestling close, heads hung together whispering.

So soon to die and wither with the spring,
Lying asleep, in unison, until February calls
Them to enhance her own forlorn and tattered self;
Then will they rise again, with the fruits
Of their own loins, and struggle yet once more.

THE YEAR'S AWAKENING

by Thomas Hardy

How do you know that the pilgrim track
Along the belting zodiac
Swept by the sun in his seeming rounds
Is traced by now to the Fishes' bounds
And into the Ram, when weeks of cloud
Have wrapt the sky in a clammy shroud,
And never as yet a tint of spring
Has shown in the Earth's apparelling;
   O vespering bird, how do you know,
     How do you know?

How do you know, deep underground,
Hid in your bed from sight and sound,
Without a turn in temperature,
With weather life can scarce endure,
That light has won a fraction's strength,
And day put on some moments' length,
Whereof in merest rote will come,
Weeks hence, mild airs that do not numb;
   O crocus root, how do you know,
     How do you know?

CROCUSES

by May Byron

Gold flame and silver flame,
Burning through the mould,
In the east wind's scornful breath,
When the world's a-cold:
Fiery from the earth's red heart
Leap they to the light,
Gold flame and silver flame
Crocus yellow and white.

EARLY SPRING DAWN

by Ivor Gurney

Long shines the thin light of the day to north-east,
The line of blue faint known and the leaping to white;
The meadows lighten, mists lessen, but light is increased,
The sun soon will appear, and dance, leaping with light.

Now milkers hear faint through dreams first cockerel crow,
Faint yet arousing thought, soon must the milk pails be flowing.
Gone out the level sheets of mists, and see, the west row
Of elms are black on the meadow edge. Day's wind is blowing.

FIRST SIGHT OF SPRING

by John Clare

The hazel blooms in threads of crimson hue
Peep through the swelling buds and look for spring
Ere yet a white thorn leaf appears in view
Or march finds throstles pleased enough to sing
On the old touchwood tree wood peckers cling
A moment and their harsh toned notes renew
In happier mood the stockdove claps his wing
The squirrel sputters up the powdered oak
With tail cocked oer his head and ears errect
Startled to hear the woodmans understroke
And with the courage that his fears collect
He hisses fierce half malice and half glee
Leaping from branch to branch about the tree
In winters foliage moss and lichens drest

SPRING

by Christina Rossetti

Frost-locked all the winter,
Seeds, and roots, and stones of fruits,
What shall make their sap ascend
That they may put forth shoots?
Tips of tender green,
Leaf, or blade, or sheath;
Telling of the hidden life
That breaks forth underneath,
Life nursed in its grave by Death.

Blows the thaw-wind pleasantly,
Drips the soaking rain,
By fits looks down the waking sun:
Young grass springs on the plain;
Young leaves clothe early hedgerow trees;
Seeds, and roots, and stones of fruits,
Swollen with sap put forth their shoots;
Curled-headed ferns sprout in the lane;
Birds sing and pair again.

There is no time like Spring,
When life's alive in everything,
Before new nestlings sing,
Before cleft swallows speed their journey back
Along the trackless track –
God guides their wing,
He spreads their table that they nothing lack, –
Before the daisy grows a common flower,
Before the sun has power
To scorch the world up in his noontide hour.

There is no time like Spring
Like Spring that passes by;
There is no life like Spring-life born to die, –
Piercing the sod,
Clothing the uncouth clod,
Hatched in the nest,
Fledged on the windy bough,
Strong on the wing:
There is no time like Spring that passes by,
Now newly born, and now
Hastening to die.

NOW IS THE TIME

by Elizabeth Coatsworth

Now is the time
when robins call,
the fretful horse
stamps in the stall,
the cock claps wings
in orchards bare,
under the hedge
crouches the hare.

Now is the time
spring fires burn,
the air is sweet
with smouldering fern,
and through the quiet
hours of the night
the gold-eyed frogs
creak with delight.

I WATCHED A BLACKBIRD

by Thomas Hardy

I watched a blackbird on a budding sycamore
One Easter Day, when sap was stirring twigs to the core;
    I saw his tongue, and crocus-coloured bill
    Parting and closing as he turned his trill;
    Then he flew down, seized on a stem of hay,
And upped to where his building scheme was under way,
As if so sure a nest were never shaped on spray.

MARCH HARES

by Andrew Young

I made myself as a tree,
No withered leaf twirling on me;
No, not a bird that stirred my boughs,
As looking out from wizard brows
I watched those lithe and lovely forms
That raised the leaves in storms.

I watched them leap and run,
Their bodies hollowed in the sun
To thin transparency,
That I could clearly see
The shallow colour of their blood
Joyous in love's full flood.

I was content enough,
Watching that serious game of love,
That happy hunting in the wood
Where the pursuer was the more pursued,
To stand in breathless hush
With no more life myself than tree or bush.

'NOW THAT THE WINTER'S GONE'

by Thomas Carew
from The Spring

Now that the winter's gone, the earth hath lost
Her snow-white robes, and now no more the frost
Candies the grass, or casts an icy cream
Upon the silver lake, or crystal stream;
But the warm sun thaws the benumb'd earth
And makes it tender, gives a sacred birth
To the dead swallow; wakes in hollow tree
The drowsy cuckoo, and the humble-bee.
Now do a choir of chirping minstrels bring
In triumph to the world, the youthful Spring.

I WANDER'D LONELY AS A CLOUD

by William Wordsworth

I wander'd lonely as a cloud
That floats on high o'er vales and hills,
When all at once I saw a crowd,
A host of golden daffodils,
Beside the lake, beneath the trees,
Fluttering and dancing in the breeze.

Continuous as the stars that shine
And twinkle on the milky way,
They stretch'd in never-ending line
Along the margin of a bay:
Ten thousand saw I at a glance,
Tossing their heads in sprightly dance.

The waves beside them danced, but they
Out-did the sparkling waves in glee –
A poet could not but be gay
In such a jocund company!
I gazed – and gazed – but little thought
What wealth the show to me had brought.

For oft, when on my couch I lie
In vacant or in pensive mood,
They flash upon that inward eye
Which is the bliss of solitude:
And then my heart with pleasure fills,
And dances with the daffodils.

To Daffodils

by Robert Herrick

Fair Daffodils, we weep to see
You haste away so soon:
As yet the early-rising Sun
Has not attain'd his noon.
Stay, stay,
Until the hasting day
Has run
But to the Even-song;
And, having pray'd together, we
Will go with you along.

We have short time to stay, as you,
We have as short a Spring;
As quick a growth to meet decay
As you, or any thing.
We die,
As your hours do, and dry
Away,
Like the Summer's rain;
Or as the pearls of morning's dew
Ne'er to be found again.

'LOVELIEST OF TREES, THE CHERRY NOW'

by A.E. Housman
from A Shropshire Lad

Loveliest of trees, the cherry now
Is hung with bloom along the bough,
And stands about the woodland ride
  Wearing white for Eastertide.

Now, of my threescore years and ten,
  Twenty will not come again,
And take from seventy springs a score,
  It only leaves me fifty more.

And since to look at things in bloom
  Fifty springs are little room,
About the woodlands I will go
To see the cherry hung with snow.

THE TREES

by Philip Larkin

The trees are coming into leaf
Like something almost being said;
The recent buds relax and spread,
Their greenness is a kind of grief.

Is it that they are born again
And we grow old? No, they die too,
Their yearly trick of looking new
Is written down in rings of grain.

Yet still the unresting castles thresh
In fullgrown thickness every May.
Last year is dead, they seem to say,
Begin afresh, afresh, afresh.

Squirrel

by John Buxton

I saw a squirrel
Run through the wood.
By every tree
It stopped; and stood
Ready to climb,
With its paw on the trunk,
and every time
(For no danger came)
It hurried on,
And was gone.

TAPESTRY TREES

by William Morris

Oak. I am the Roof-tree and the Keel:
I bridge the seas for woe and weal.

Fir. High o'er the lordly oak I stand,
And drive him on from land to land.

Ash. I heft my brother's iron bane;
I shaft the spear and build the wain.

Yew. Dark down the windy dale I grow,
The father of the fateful Bow.

Poplar. The war-shaft and the milking-bowl
I make, and keep the hay-wain whole.

Olive. The King I bless; the lamps I trim;
In my warm wave do fishes swim.

Apple-tree. I bowed my head to Adam's will;
The cups of toiling men I fill.

Vine. I draw the blood from out the earth:
I store the sun for winter mirth.

Orange-tree. Amidst the greenness of my night
My odorous lamps hang round and bright.

Fig-tree. I who am little among trees
In honey-making mate the bees.

Mulberry-tree. Love's lack hath dyed my berries red:
For Love's attire my leaves are shed.

Pear-tree. High o'er the mead-flowers' hidden feet
I bear aloft my burden sweet.

Bay. Look on my leafy boughs, the Crown
Of living song and dead renown!

23

'WAK'D BY HIS WARMER RAY, THE REPTILE YOUNG'

by James Thomson
from The Seasons

Wak'd by his warmer ray, the reptile young
Come wing'd abroad; by the light air upborne,
Lighter, and full of soul. From every chink,
And secret corner, where they slept away
The wintry storms; or rising from their tombs,
To higher life; by myriads, forth at once,
Swarming they pour; all of the vary'd hues
Their beauty-beaming parent can disclose,
Ten thousand forms, ten thousand different tribes,
People the blaze. To sunny waters some
By fatal instinct fly; where on the pool
They, sportive, wheel: or, sailing down the stream,
Are snatch'd immediate by the quick-ey'd trout,
Or darting salmon. Through the green-wood glade
Some love to stray; there lodg'd, amus'd, and fed,
In the fresh leaf. Luxurious, others make
The meads of their choice, and visit every flower,
And every latent herb: for the sweet task,
To propagate their kinds, and where to wrap,
In what soft beds, their young yet undisclos'd,
Employs their tender care. Some to the house,
The fold, and dairy, hungry, bed their flight;
Sip round the pail, or taste the curdling cheese;
Oft, inadvertent, from the milky stream
They meet their fate; or, weltering in the bowl,
With powerless wings around them wrapt, expire.

THE BLUEBELL

by Anne Brontë

A fine and subtle spirit dwells
  In every little flower
Each one its own sweet feeling breathes
  With more or less of power.

There is a silent eloquence
  In every wild bluebell,
That fills my softened heart with bliss
  That words could never tell.

'BIRDS I BEHELD BUILDING NESTS IN THE BUSHES'

by *William Langland*
from *Piers the Plowman*
Passus XI (B Text, ll. 336–53)

Birds I beheld building nests in the bushes
Which no man had the wit even to begin to work.
I wondered where and from whom the pie could have learned
To put together the sticks in which she lays and broods,
For there is no craftsman, I know, who could construct her
    nest,
And it would be a wonder if any mason had made such a mould.
    And yet I marvelled even more at how many birds
Concealed their eggs which were carefully secreted
In marshes and moors so that men could not find them,
And their eggs lay hidden when they flew up in fear
Because of other birds or of beasts of prey.
And some trod their mates and bred in the trees
And brought forth their broods high up from the ground,
And some conceived by breathing through their beaks,
And others coupled, and I took note how the peacocks bred.
I marvelled much over what master they could have had,
And who taught them to timber so high in the trees,
Where neither man nor beast could get near their birds.

Translated by Peggy Munsterberg

THE THRUSH'S NEST

by John Clare

Within a thick and spreading hawthorn bush
That overhung a molehill large and round
I heard from morn to morn a merry thrush
Sing hymns to sunrise, while I drank the sound
With joy and, often an intruding guest,
I watched her secret toils from day to day
How true she warped the moss to form her nest
And modelled it within with wood and clay
And bye and bye like heath bells gilt with dew
There lay her shining eggs as bright as flowers
Ink-spotted over shells of greeny blue
And there I witnessed in the summer hours
A brood of natures minstrels chirp and fly
Glad as the sunshine and the laughing sky

CUCKOOS

by Andrew Young

When coltsfoot withers and begins to wear
Long silver locks instead of golden hair,
And fat red catkins from black poplars fall
And on the ground like caterpillars crawl,
And bracken lifts up slender arms and wrists
And stretches them, unfolding sleepy fists,
The cuckoos in a few well-chosen words
Tell they give Easter eggs to the small birds.

27

WRITTEN IN MARCH
while RESTING ON THE BRIDGE
AT THE FOOT OF
BROTHER'S WATER

by William Wordsworth

The cock is crowing,
The stream is flowing,
The small birds twitter,
The lake doth glitter,
The green field sleeps in the sun;
The oldest and youngest
Are at work with the strongest;
The cattle are grazing,
Their heads never raising;
There are forty feeding like one!

Like an army defeated
The snow hath retreated,
And now doth fare ill
On top of the bare hill;
The ploughboy is whooping – anon – anon:
There's joy in the mountains;
There's life in the fountains;
Small clouds are sailing,
Blue sky prevailing;
The rain is over and gone!

'Spring is the season when the young things thrive'

by *Vita Sackville-West*
from *The Land*

Spring is the season when the young things thrive,
Having the kindly months before them. Lambs,
Already sturdy, straggle from the flock;
Frisk tails; tug grass-tufts; stare at children; prance;
Then panic-stricken scuttle for their dams.
Calves learn to drink from buckets; foals
Trot laxly in the meadow, with soft glance
Inquisitive; barn, sty and shed
Teem with young innocence newly come alive.
Round collie puppies, on the sunny step,
Buffet each other with their duffer paws
And pounce at flies, and nose the plaited skep,
And with tucked tail slink yelping from the hive.
Likewise the little secret beasts
That open eyes on a world of death and dread,
Thirst, hunger, and mishap,
The covert denizens of holts and shaws,
The little creatures of the ditch and hedge,
Mice nested in a tussock, shrews, and voles,
Inhabitants of the wood,
The red-legged dabchick, paddling in the sedge,
Followed by chubby brood;
The vixen, prick-eared for the first alarm
Beside her tumbling cubs at foot of tree, –
All in the spring begin their precarious round,
Not cherished as the striplings on the farm,
Sheltered, and cosseted, and kept from harm,
But fang and claw against them, snare and trap,
For life is perilous to the small wild things,
Danger's their lot, and fears abound . . .

EASTER

by William Drummond of Hawthornden

All-bearing Earth, like a new-married queen,
Her beauties heightens in a gown of green;
Perfumes the air; her meads are wrought with flowers;
In colours various, figures, smelling, powers;
Trees wanton in the groves with leafy locks;
Here hills enamell'd stand; the vales, the rocks,
Ring peals of joy; here floods and prattling brooks
(Stars' liquid mirrors), with serpenting crooks,
And whispering murmurs, sound unto the main, –
'The golden age returned is again!'
The honey people leave their golden bowers,
And innocently prey on budding flowers;
In gloomy shades, perch'd on the tender sprays,
The painted singers fill the air with lays.

WATER COLOURS

by Ivor Gurney

The trembling water glimpsed through dark tangle
Of late-month April's delicatest thorn,
One moment put the cuckoo-flower to scorn
Where its head hangs by sedges, Severn bank-full.
But dark water has a hundred fires on it;
As the sky changes it changes and ranges through
Sky colours and thorn colours, and more would do,
Were not the blossom truth so quick on it,
And beauty brief in action as first dew.

30

HOME-THOUGHTS, FROM ABROAD

by Robert Browning

Oh, to be in England,
Now that April's there,
And whoever wakes in England
Sees, some morning, unaware,
That the lowest boughs and the brushwood sheaf
Round the elm-tree bole are in tiny leaf,
While the chaffinch sings on the orchard bough
In England – now!

And after April, when May follows,
And the whitethroat builds, and all the swallows!
Hark, where my blossomed pear-tree in the hedge
Leans to the field and scatters on the clover
Blossoms and dewdrops – at the bent spray's edge –
That's the wise thrush; he sings each song twice over,
Lest you should think he never could recapture
The first fine careless rapture!
And though the fields look rough with hoary dew
And will be gay when noontide wakes anew
The buttercups, the little children's dower
– Far brighter than this gaudy melon-flower!

from THE LARK ASCENDING

by George Meredith

He rises and begins to round,
He drops the silver chain of sound,
Of many links without a break,
In chirrup, whistle, slur and shake,
All intervolved and spreading wide,
Like water-dimples down a tide
Where ripple ripple overcurls
And eddy into eddy whirls;
A press of hurried notes that run
So fleet they scarce are more than one,
Yet changeingly the trills repeat
And linger ringing while they fleet,
Sweet to the quick o' the ear, and dear
To her beyond the handmaid ear,
Who sits beside our inner springs,
Too often dry for this he brings,
Which seems the very jet of earth
At sight of sun, her music's mirth,
As up he wings the spiral stair,
A song of light, and pierces air
With fountain ardour, fountain play,
To reach the shining tops of day,
And drink in everything discerned
An ecstasy to music turned,
Impelled by what his happy bill
Disperses; drinking, showering still,
Unthinking save that he may give
His voice the outlet, there to live

Renewed in endless notes of glee,
So thirsty of his voice is he,
For all to hear and all to know
That he is joy, awake, aglow,
The tumult of the heart to hear
Through pureness filtered crystal-clear,
And know the pleasure sprinkled bright
By simple singing of delight,
Shrill, irreflective, unrestrained,
Rapt, ringing, on the jet sustained
Without a break, without a fall,
Sweet-silvery, sheer lyrical,
Perennial, quavering up the chord
Like myriad dews of sunny sward
That trembling into fulness shine,
And sparkle dropping argentine;
Such wooing as the ear receives
From zephyr caught in choric leaves
Of aspens when their chattering net
Is flushed to white with shivers wet;
And such the water-spirit's chime
On mountain heights in morning's prime,
Too freshly sweet to seem excess,
Too animate to need a stress;
But wider over many heads
The starry voice ascending spreads,
Awakening, as it waxes thin,
The best in us to him akin;

And every face to watch him raised,
Puts on the light of children praised,
So rich our human pleasure ripes
When sweetness on sincereness pipes,
Though nought be promised from the seas,
But only a soft-ruffling breeze
Sweep glittering on a still content,
Serenity in ravishment.
For singing till his heaven fills,
'Tis love of earth that he instils,
And ever winging up and up,
Our valley is his golden cup,
And he the wine which overflows
To lift us with him as he goes:
The woods and brooks, the sheep and kine,
He is, the hills, the human line,
The meadows green, the fallows brown,
The dreams of labour in the town;
He sings the sap, the quickened veins;
The wedding song of sun and rains
He is, the dance of children, thanks
Of sowers, shout of primrose-banks,
And eye of violets while they breathe;
All these the circling song will wreathe,
And you shall hear the herb and tree,
The better heart of men shall see,
Shall feel celestially, as long
As you crave nothing save the song.

M A Y

by *Peter Forbes*
from *The Aerial Noctiluca*

May comes up with tit-show
May comes up with a sneeze
May slips by with a whiff and a sigh
Blossom on the breeze

May comes up with windows
May lolls bare at ease
May burns brown as the sun goes down
Curtains in the breeze

May comes up with bunting
May was born to please
May rides high with a billowing sky
Candles on the trees

May comes up with visions
May knows how to tease
May goes by in the blink of an eye
Flaunting dappled dreams

THE CATERPILLAR

by Christina Rossetti

Brown and furry
Caterpillar in a hurry,
Take your walk
To the shady leaf, or stalk,
  Or what not
Which may be the chosen spot.
  No toad spy on you,
Hovering bird of prey pass by you;
Spin and die,
To live again a butterfly.

THE HILL PINES WERE SIGHING

by Robert Bridges

The hill pines were sighing,
O'ercast and chill was the day:
A mist in the valley lying
Blotted the pleasant May.

But deep in the glen's bosom
Summer slept in the fire
Of the odorous gorse-blossom
And the hot scent of the brier.

A ribald cuckoo clamoured,
And out of the copse the stroke
Of the iron axe that hammered
The iron heart of the oak.

Anon a sound appalling,
As a hundred years of pride
Crashed, in the silence falling:
And the shadowy pine-trees sighed.

THE VILLAIN

by W.H. Davies

While joy gave clouds the light of stars,
    That beamed where'er they looked;
And calves and lambs had tottering knees,
    Excited, while they sucked;
While every bird enjoyed his song,
Without one thought of harm or wrong –
I turned my head and saw the wind,
    Nor far from where I stood,
Dragging the corn by her golden hair,
    Into a dark and lonely wood.

'How calm, how beautiful, comes on'

by Thomas Moore
from Lalla Rookh

How calm, how beautiful, comes on
The stilly hour, when storms are gone;
When warring winds have died away,
And clouds, beneath the glancing ray,
Melt off, and leave the land and sea
Sleeping in bright tranquillity, –
Fresh as if Day again were born,
Again upon the lap of Morn!
When the light blossoms, rudely torn
And scattered at the whirlwind's will,
Hang floating in the pure air still,
Filling it all with precious balm,
In gratitude for this sweet calm; –
And every drop the thunder-showers
Have left upon the grass and flowers
Sparkles, as 'twere the lightning-gem
Whose liquid flame is born of them!

SPRING GOETH ALL IN WHITE

by Robert Bridges

Spring goeth all in white,
Crowned with milk-white may:
In fleecy flocks of light
O'er heaven the white clouds stray:

White butterflies in the air;
White daisies prank the ground:
The cherry and hoary pear
Scatter their snow around.

I BENDED UNTO ME

by T.E. Brown

I bended unto me a bough of May,
That I might see and smell:
It bore it in a sort of way,
It bore it very well.
But, when I let it backward sway,
Then it were hard to tell
With what a toss, with what a swing,
The dainty thing
Resumed its proper level,
And sent me to the devil.
I know it did — you doubt it?
I turned, and saw them whispering about it.

To Blossoms

by Robert Herrick

Fair pledges of a fruitful tree,
Why do ye fall so fast?
Your date is not so past,
But you may stay yet here awhile,
To blush and gently smile;
And go at last.

What, were ye born to be
An hour or half's delight;
And so to bid good-night?
'Twas pity Nature brought ye forth
Merely to show your worth,
And lose you quite.

But you are lovely leaves, where we
May read how soon things have
Their end, though ne'er so brave:
And after they have shown their pride
Like you, awhile, they glide
Into the grave.

'THESE FLOW'RS WHITE AND RED'

by Geoffrey Chaucer
from The Prologue to
The Legend of Good Women

These flow'rs white and red,
Such that men callen daisies in our town;
To them have I so great affection,
As I said erst, when comen is the May,
That in my bed there dawneth me no day
That I n'am up and walking in the mead
To see this flow'r against the sunne spread,
When it upriseth early by the morrow;
That blissful sight softeneth all my sorrow
So glad am I, when that I have presence
Of it, to doen it all reverence.

THE SERPENT

by Percy Bysshe Shelley

Wake the serpent not – lest he
Should not know the way to go –
Let him crawl which yet lies sleeping
Through the deep grass of the meadow!
Not a bee shall hear him creeping,
Not a may-fly shall awaken
From its cradling blue-bell shaken,
Not the starlight as he's sliding
Through the grass with silent gliding.

Spring

by Henry Howard, Earl of Surrey

Wherein each thing renews, save only the Lover

The soote season, that bud and bloom forth brings,
With green hath clad the hill and eke the vale:
The nightingale with feathers new she sings;
The turtle to her make hath told her tale.
Summer is come, for every spray now springs:
The hart hath held his old head on the pale;
The buck in brake his winter coat he flings;
The fishes flete with new repairèd scale.
The adder all her slough away she slings;
The swift swallow pursueth the flies smale;
The busy bee her honey now she mings;
Winter is worn that was the flowers bale.
And thus I see among these pleasant things
Each care decays, and yet my sorrow springs.

'ALL-BEAUTEOUS NATURE! BY THY BOUNDLESS CHARMS'

by Joseph Warton
from The Enthusiast

All-beauteous Nature! by thy boundless charms
Oppress'd, O where shall I begin thy praise,
Where turn th'ecstatic eye, how ease my breast
That pants with wild astonishment and love!
Dark forests, and the opening lawn, refresh'd
With ever-gushing brooks, hill, meadow, dale,
The balmy bean-field, the gay-clover'd close,
So sweetly interchang'd, the lowing ox,
The playful lamb, the distant water-fall
Now faintly heard, now swelling with the breeze;
The sound of pastoral reed from hazel-bower,
The choral birds, the neighing steed, that snuffs
His dappled mate, stung with intense desire;
The ripen'd orchard when the ruddy orbs
Betwixt the green leaves blush, the azure skies,
The cheerful sun that through earth's vitals pours
Delight and health and heat; all, all conspire
To raise, to sooth, to harmonize the mind,
To lift on wings of praise, to the great Sire
Of being and of beauty . . .

THE WILLOW

by Walter de la Mare

Leans now the fair willow, dreaming
Amid her locks of green.
In the driving snow she was parch'd and cold,
And in midnight hath been
Swept by blasts of the void night,
Lashed by the rains.
Now of that wintry dark and bleak
No memory remains.

In mute desire she sways softly;
Thrilling sap up-flows;
She praises God in her beauty and grace,
Whispers delight. And there flows
A delicate wind from the Southern seas,
Kissing her leaves. She sighs.
While the birds in her tresses make merry;
Burns the Sun in the skies.

A MILL

by William Allingham

Two leaps the water from its race
    Made to the brook below,
The first leap it was curving glass,
    The second bounding snow.

'MARK WELL THE VARIOUS SEASONS OF THE YEAR'

by John Gay
from *Rural Sports: A Georgic*

Mark well the various seasons of the year,
How the succeeding insect race appear;
In this revolving moon one colour reigns,
Which in the next the fickle trout disdains.
Oft have I seen a skilful angler try
The various colours of the treach'rous fly;
When he with fruitless pain hath skimm'd the brook,
And the coy fish rejects the skipping hook,
He shakes the boughs that on the margin grow,
Which o'er the stream a waving forest throw;
When if an insect fall (his certain guide)
He gently takes him from the whirling tide;
Examines well his form with curious eyes,
His gaudy vest, his wings, his horns and size,
Then round his hook the chosen fur he winds,
And on the back a speckled feather binds,
So just the colours shine thro' every part,
That nature seems to live again in art.
Let not thy wary step advance too near,
While all thy hope hangs on a single hair;
The new-form'd insect on the water moves,
The speckled trout the curious snare approves;
Upon the curling surface let it glide,
With nat'ral motion from thy hand supplied,
Against the stream now let it gently play,
Now in the rapid eddy roll away.
The scaly shoals float by, and seiz'd with fear
Behold their fellows toss'd in thinner air;
But soon they leap, and catch the swimming bait,
Plunge on the hook, and share an equal fate.

TROUT

by Seamus Heaney

Hangs, a fat gun-barrel,
deep under arched bridges
or slips like butter down
the throat of the river.

From depths smooth-skinned as plums
his muzzle gets bull's eye;
picks off grass-seed and moths
that vanish, torpedoed.

Where water unravels
over gravel-beds he
is fired from the shallows
white belly reporting

flat; darts like a tracer-
bullet back between stones
and is never burnt out.
A volley of cold blood

ramrodding the current.

THE ANGLER'S WISH

by Izaak Walton
from *The Compleat Angler*

I in these flowery meads would be;
These crystal streams should solace me;
To whose harmonious bubbling noise,
I with my angle will rejoice;
Sit here, and see the turtle-dove
Court his chaste mate to acts of love.

Or on the bank feel the west wind
Breathe health and plenty; please my mind
To see sweet dewdrops kiss these flowers,
And then wash'd off by April showers;
Here, here my Kenna sing a song;
There, see a blackbird feed her young.

Or, a laverock build her nest:
Here, give my weary spirits rest,
And raise my low-pitch'd thoughts above
Earth, or what poor mortals love:
Thus, free from lawsuits and the noise
Of princes' courts, I would rejoice.

Or, with my Bryan and a book,
Loiter long days near Shawford brook;
There sit with him and eat my meat,
There see the sun both rise and set,
There bid good-morning to each day,
There meditate my time away,
And angle on: and beg to have
A quiet passage to a welcome grave.

from ON WESTWALL DOWNES
(Extracts)

by William Strode

When Westwall Downes I gan to tread,
Where cleanely wynds the greene did sweepe,
Methought a landskipp there was spread,
Here a bush and there a sheepe:
    The pleated wrinkles of the face
    Of wave-swolne earth did lend such grace,
    As shadowings in Imag'ry
    Which both deceive and please the eye.

The sheepe sometymes did tread the maze
By often wynding in and in,
And sometimes round about they trace
Which mylkmaydes call a Fairie ring:
    Such semicircles have they runne,
    Such lynes across so trymly spunne
    That sheppeards learne whenere they please
    A new Geometry with ease.

Here and there twoe hilly crests
Amiddst them hugg a pleasant greene,
And these are like twoe swelling breasts
That close a tender fall betweene.
    Here would I sleepe, or read, or pray
    From early morn till flight of day:
    But harke! a sheepe-bell calls mee upp,
    Like Oxford colledge bells, to supp.

CONSIDERING THE SNAIL

by Thom Gunn

The snail pushes through a green
night, for the grass is heavy
with water and meets over
the bright path he makes, where rain
has darkened the earth's dark. He
moves in a wood of desire,

pale antlers barely stirring
as he hunts. I cannot tell
what power is at work, drenched there
with purpose, knowing nothing.
What is a snail's fury? All
I think is that if later

I parted the blades above
the tunnel and saw the thin
trail of broken white across
litter, I would never have
imagined the slow passion
to that deliberate progress.

EARTH TO EARTH

by John Davidson

Where the region grows without a lord,
   Between the thickets emerald-stored,
In the woodland bottom the virgin sward,
   The cream of the earth, through depths of mold
   O'erflowing wells from secret cells,
While the moon and the sun keep watch and ward,
   And the ancient world is never old.

Here, alone, by the grass-green hearth
   Tarry a little: the mood will come!
Feel your body a part of the earth;
   Rest and quicken your thought at home;
     Take your ease with the brooding trees;
Join in their deep-down silent mirth
   The crumbling rock and the fertile loam.

Listen and watch! The wind will sing;
   And the day go out by the western gate;
The night come up on her darkling wing;
   And the stars with flaming torches wait.
     Listen and see! And love and be
The day and the night and the world-wide thing
   Of strength and hope you contemplate.

A Day in Sussex

by *Wilfrid Scawen Blunt*
from *The Love Sonnets of Proteus*
(Part IV: Vita Nova)

The dove did lend me wings. I fled away
From the loud world which long had troubled me.
Oh lightly did I flee when hoyden May
Threw her wild mantle on the hawthorn-tree.
I left the dusty high road, and my way
Was through deep meadows, shut with copses fair.
A choir of thrushes poured its roundelay
From every hedge and every thicket there.
Mild, moon-faced kine looked on, where in the grass
All heaped with flowers I lay, from noon till eve.
And hares unwitting close to me did pass,
And still the birds sang, and I could not grieve.
Oh what a blessed thing that evening was!
Peace, music, twilight, all that could deceive
A soul to joy or lull a heart to peace.
It glimmers yet across whole years like these.

'LOVELY ARE THE CURVES OF THE WHITE OWL SWEEPING'

by *George Meredith*
from *Love in the Valley*

Lovely are the curves of the white owl sweeping
Wavy in the dusk lit by one large star.
Lone on the fir-branch, his rattle-note unvaried,
Brooding o'er the gloom, spins the brown eve-jar.

'NOW CAME STILL EVENING ON, AND TWILIGHT GREY'

by *John Milton*
from *Paradise Lost*
(Book IV)

Now came still evening on, and twilight grey
Had in her sober livery all things clad;
Silence accompanied, for beast and bird,
They to their grassy couch, these to their nests
Were slunk, all but the wakeful nightingale;
She all night long her amorous descant sung;
Silence was pleased: now glowed the firmament
With living sapphires: Hesperus that led
The starry host, rode brightest, till the moon
Rising in clouded majesty, at length,
Apparent queen, unveiled her peerless light,
And o'er the dark her silver mantle threw.

53

TWO PEWITS

by Edward Thomas

Under the after-sunset sky
Two pewits sport and cry,
More white than is the moon on high
Riding the dark surge silently;
More black than earth. Their cry
Is the one sound under the sky.
They alone move, now low, now high,
And merrily they cry
To the mischievous Spring sky,
Plunging earthward, tossing high,
Over the ghost who wonders why
So merrily they cry and fly,
Nor choose 'twixt earth and sky,
While the moon's quarter silently
Rides, and earth rests as silently.

OF THE GOING DOWN OF THE SUN

by John Bunyan

What, hast thou run thy Race? Are going down?
Thou seemest angry, why dost on us frown?
Yea wrap thy head with Clouds, and hide thy face,
As threatning to withdraw from us thy Grace?
Oh leave us not! When once thou hid'st thy head,
Our Hórizon with darkness will be spread.
Tell's, who hath thee offended? Turn again:
Alas! too late – Entreaties are in vain! . . .

'HOW BEAUTIFUL IS NIGHT'

by Robert Southey
from *Thalaba*
(Book 1, stanza 1)

How beautiful is night!
    A dewy freshness fills the silent air;
No mist obscures, nor cloud, nor speck, nor stain,
    Breaks the serene of heaven;
  In full-orbed glory yonder moon divine
  Rolls through the dark blue depths.
    Beneath her steady ray
    The desert-circle spreads,
  Like the round ocean, girdled with the sky.
    How beautiful is night!

THE MOTH

by Walter de la Mare

Isled in the midnight air,
Musked with the dark's faint bloom,
Out into the glooming and secret haunts
  The flame cries, 'Come!'

Lovely in dye and fan,
A-tremble in shimmering grace,
A moth from her winter swoon
  Uplifts her face:

Stares from her glamorous eyes;
Wafts her on plumes like mist;
In ecstasy swirls and sways
  To her strange tryst.

'IN SUCH A NIGHT, WHEN PASSING CLOUDS GIVE PLACE'

by Anne, Countess of Winchilsea
from A Nocturnal Reverie

In such a night, when passing clouds give place,
Or thinly veil the heaven's mysterious face;
When in some river overhung with green,
The waving moon and trembling leaves are seen;
When fresh'ned grass now bears itself upright,
And makes cool banks to pleasing rest invite,
Whence springs the woodbine and the bramble-rose,
And where the sleepy cowslip shelter'd grows;
Whilst now a paler hue the foxglove takes,
Yet chequers still with red the dusky brakes;
When scatter'd glow-worms, but in twilight fine,
Show trivial beauties, watch their hour to shine.

ELEGIAC SONNET

by Charlotte Smith

The garlands fade that Spring so lately wove,
  Each simple flower, which she had nurs'd in dew,
Anemonies, that spangled every grove,
  The primrose wan, and hare-bell mildly blue.
No more shall violets linger in the dell,
  Or purple orchis variegate the plain,
Till Spring again shall call forth every bell,
  And dress with humid hands her wreaths again.
Ah! poor humanity! so frail, so fair,
  Are the fond visions of thy early day,
Till tyrant passion, and corrosive care,
  Bid all thy fairy colours fade away!
Another May new buds and flowers shall bring;
  Ah! why has happiness – no second Spring?

SUMMER

'Now welcome, summer, with thy sunne soft,
That has this winter's weather overshake,
And driven away the longe nightes black!

'Saint Valentine that art full high on loft
Thus singen smalle fowles for thy sake:
Now welcome, summer, with thy sunne soft
That has this winter's weather overshake.'

from *The Parliament of Birds*
Geoffrey Chaucer

WRITTEN ON THE LONGEST DAY OF THE YEAR WHICH WAS GIVEN TO CHERRY-PICKING

Anonymous

The moon high and dry
In the five o'clock sky
Shows a feather-pale face
As the sun joins the chase
Rising hot from his bed –
Though broad shade is spread
Of trees on the grass
The dews are soon fled
From the sky's burning glass.

Now silent for long
Is birds' early song:
But rooks in a ring
And clacking starling
With sparrows and thrushes
From field and from bushes
Now flock to the cherries
To bill the rich berries
Before the bright sun
Wakes the man with the gun.

SKIES OF EARLY MORNING

by Ann Leo

Skies of early morning,
Purple and blue,
Grey tinged,
Blends true,
Forecasts sunny day
As pale blue and pale green mingle,
Trees reach up arms to Heaven,
Every great tree pure and single,
Voices of early morn reach my ears,
Corn-sheafs in the fields rustle golden spears,
The birds trill sweetest notes,
Pure golden notes of loving thought,
While bright light struggles thro' the coats
Of purple cloud and peeps between
The breast of early morning sky.
Perhaps at so early an hour
The light of day is shy.

from THE ENTAIL, A FABLE

by Horace Walpole

In a fair Summer's radiant morn
A Butterfly, divinely born,
Whose lineage dated from the mud
Of Noah's or Deucalion's flood,
Long hov'ring round a perfum'd lawn,
By various gusts of odours drawn,
At last establish'd his repose
On the rich bosom of a Rose.
The palace pleas'd the lordly guest:
What insect own'd a prouder nest?

'SO, SOME TEMPESTUOUS MORN IN EARLY JUNE'

by Matthew Arnold
from Thyrsis

So, some tempestuous morn in early June,
    When the year's primal burst of bloom is o'er,
        Before the roses and the longest day –
    When garden-walks, and all the grassy floor,
        With blossoms, red and white, of fallen May,
            And chestnut-flowers are strewn –
So have I heard the cuckoo's parting cry,
    From the wet field, through the vext garden-trees,
    Come with the volleying rain and tossing breeze:
    The bloom is gone, and with the bloom go I.

Too quick despairer, wherefore wilt thou go?
    Soon will the high Midsummer pomps come on,
        Soon will the musk carnations break and swell,
    Soon shall we have gold-dusted snapdragon,
        Sweet-William with its homely cottage-smell,
            And stocks in fragrant blow;
    Roses that down the alleys shine afar,
        And open, jasmine-muffled lattices,
        And groups under the dreaming garden-trees,
And the full moon, and the white evening-star.

'ALONG THESE BLUSHING BORDERS, BRIGHT WITH DEW'

by *James Thomson*
from *The Seasons*

Along these blushing borders, bright with dew,
And in yon mingled wilderness of flowers,
Fair-handed Spring unbosoms every grace;
Throws out the snowdrop, and the crocus first;
The daisy, primrose, violet darkly blue,
And polyanthus of unnumber'd dyes;
The yellow wall-flower, stain'd with iron brown;
And lavish stock that scents the garden round:
From the soft wing of vernal breezes shed,
Anemonies; auriculas, enrich'd
With shining meal o'er all their velvet leaves;
And full ranunculas, of glowing red.
Then comes the tulip-race, where Beauty plays
Her idle freaks; from family diffus'd
To family, as flies the father dust,
The varied colours run; and, while they break
On the charm'd eye, th'exulting florist marks,
With secret pride, the wonders of his hand.
No gradual bloom is wanting; from the bud,
First-born of Spring, to Summer's musky tribes;
Nor hyacinths, of purest virgin white,
Low-bent, and blushing inward; nor jonquilles,
Of potent fragrance; nor narcissus fair,
As o'er the fabled fountain hanging still;
Nor broad carnations, nor gay-spotted pinks;
Nor, shower'd from every bush, the damask rose.
Infinite numbers, delicacies, smells,
With hues on hues expression cannot paint,
The breath of Nature, and her endless bloom.

from **THE STUDY OF A SPIDER**

by John Leicester Warren, Lord de Tabley

From holy flower to holy flower
Thou weavest thine unhallowed bower.
The harmless dewdrops, beaded thin,
Ripple along thy ropes of sin.
Thy house a grave, a gulf thy throne
Affright the fairies every one.
Thy winding sheets are grey and fell,
Inprisoning with nets of hell
The lovely births that winnow by,
Winged sisters of the rainbow sky:
Elf-darlings, fluffy, bee-bright things,
And owl-white moths with mealy wings,
And tiny flies, as gauzy thin
As e'er were shut electrum in.
These are thy death spoils, insect ghoul,
With their dear life thy fangs are foul.
Thou felon anchorite of pain
Who sittest in a world of slain.
Hermit, who tunest song unsweet
To heaving wing and writhing feet.
A glutton of creation's sighs,
Miser of many miseries.
Toper, whose lonely feasting chair
Sways in inhospitable air.
The board is bare, the bloated host
Drinks to himself toast after toast.
His lip requires no goblet brink,
But like a weasel must he drink.
The vintage is as old as time
And bright as sunset, pressed and prime.

66

A FINE DAY

by Michael Drayton

Clear had the day been from the dawn,
All chequer'd was the sky,
Thin clouds like scarfs of cobweb lawn
Veil'd heaven's most glorious eye.
The wind had no more strength than this,
That leisurely it blew,
To make one leaf the next to kiss
That closely by it grew.

JUNE

by Francis Ledwidge

Broom out the floor now, lay the fender by,
And plant this bee-sucked bough of woodbine there,
And let the window down. The butterfly
Floats in upon the sunbeam, and the fair
Tanned face of June, the nomad gipsy, laughs
Above her widespread wares, the while she tells
The farmers' fortunes in the fields, and quaffs
The water from the spider-peopled wells.

The hedges are all drowned in green grass seas,
And bobbing poppies flare like Elmo's light,
While siren-like the pollen-stained bees
Drone in the clover depths. And up the height
The cuckoo's voice is hoarse and broke with joy.
And on the lowland crops the crows make raid,
Nor fear the clappers of the farmer's boy,
Who sleeps, like drunken Noah, in the shade.

And loop this red rose in that hazel ring
That snares your little ear, for June is short
And we must joy in it and dance and sing,
And from her bounty draw her rosy worth.
Ay! soon the swallows will be flying south,
The wind wheel north to gather in the snow,
Even the roses spilt in youth's red mouth
Will soon blow down the road all roses go.

SWEENEY PRAISES THE TREES

Anonymous

The branchy leafy oak-tree
is highest in the wood,
the shooting hazel bushes
hide sweet hazel-nuts.

The alder is my darling,
all thornless in the gap,
some milk of human kindness
coursing in its sap.

The blackthorn is a jaggy creel,
stippled with dark sloes;
green watercress is thatch on wells
where the drinking blackbird goes.

Sweetest of the leafy stalks,
the vetches strew the pathway;
the oyster-grass is my delight
and the wild strawberry.

Low-set clumps of apple-trees
drum down fruit when shaken;
scarlet berries clot like blood
on mountain rowan.

Briars curl in sideways,
arch a stickle back,
draw blood, and curl back innocent
to sneak the next attack.

The yew-tree in each churchyard
wraps night in its dark hood.
ivy is a shadowy
genius of the wood.

Holly rears its windbreak,
a door in winter's face;
life-blood on a spear-shaft
darkens the grain of ash.

Birch-tree, smooth and pale-skinned,
delicious to the breeze,
high twigs plait and crown it
the queen of trees.

The aspen pales
and whispers, hesitates:
a thousand frightened scuts
race in its leaves.

But what disturbs me most
in the living wood
is the swishing to and fro
of an oak-rod.

Translated from the Irish by
Seamus Heaney

Starlings

by *Norman MacCaig*

Can you keep it so,
cool tree, making a blue cage
for an obstreperous population? –
for a congregation of mediaeval scholars
quarrelling in several languages? –
for busybodies marketing
in the bazaar of green leaves? –
for clockwork fossils that can't be still even
when the Spring runs down?

No tree, no blue cage can contain
that restlessness. They whirr off
and sow themselves in a scattered handful
on the grass – and are
bustling monks
tilling their green precincts.

from THERE IS A HILL

by Robert Bridges

There is a hill beside the silver Thames,
　Shady with birch and beech and odorous pine:
And brilliant underfoot with thousand gems
Steeply the thickets to his floods decline.
　Straight trees in every place
　Their thick tops interlace,
And pendant branches trail their foliage fine
　Upon his watery face.

Swift from the sweltering pasturage he flows:
His stream, alert to seek the pleasant shade,
Pictures his gentle purpose, as he goes
Straight to the caverned pool his toil has made.
　His winter floods lay bare
　The stout roots in the air:
His summer streams are cool, when they have played
　Among their fibrous hair.

A rushy island guards the sacred bower,
And hides it from the meadow, where in peace
The lazy cows wrench many a scented flower,
Robbing the golden market of the bees:
　And laden barges float
　By banks of myosote;
And scented flag and golden flower-de-lys
　Delay the loitering boat.

And on this side the island, where the pool
Eddies away, are tangled mass on mass
The water-weeds, that net the fishes cool,
And scarce allow a narrow stream to pass;
    Where spreading crowfoot mars
    The drowning nenuphars,
Waving the tassels of her silken grass
    Below her silver stars.

But in the purple pool there nothing grows,
Not the white water-lily spoked with gold;
Though best she loves the hollows, and well knows
On quiet streams her broad shields to unfold:
    Yet should her roots but try
    Within these deeps to lie,
Not her long-reaching stalk could ever hold
    Her waxen head so high.

Sometimes an angler comes, and drops his hook
Within its hidden depths, and 'gainst a tree
Leaning his rod, reads in some pleasant book,
Forgetting soon his pride of fishery;
    And dreams, or falls asleep,
    While curious fishes peep
About his nibbled bait, or scornfully
    Dart off and rise and leap.

THE KINGFISHER

by W.H. Davies

It was the Rainbow gave thee birth,
  And left thee all her lovely hues;
And, as her mother's name was Tears,
  So runs it in my blood to choose
For haunts the lonely pools, and keep
In company with trees that weep.

Go you and, with such glorious hues,
  Live with proud Peacocks in green parks;
On lawns as smooth as shining glass,
  Let every feather show its marks;
Get thee on boughs and clap thy wings
Before the windows of proud kings.

Nay, lovely Bird, thou art not vain;
  Thou hast no proud, ambitious mind;
I also love a quiet place
  That's green, away from all mankind;
A lonely pool, and let a tree
Sigh with her bosom over me.

THE TROUT

by John Montague

Flat on the bank I parted
Rushes to ease my hands
In the water without a ripple
And tilt them slowly downstream
To where he lay, light as a leaf,
In his fluid sensual dream.

Bodiless lord of creation
I hung briefly above him
Savouring my own absence
Senses expanding in the slow
Motion, the photographic calm
That grows before action.

As the curve of my hands
Swung under his body
He surged, with visible pleasure.
I was so preternaturally close
I could count every stipple
But still cast no shadow, until

The two palms crossed in a cage
Under the lightly pulsing gills.
Then (entering my own enlarged
Shape, which rode on the water)
I gripped. To this day I can
Taste his terror on my hands.

'AND BRIGHT AND SILVERY THE WILLOWS SLEEP'

by Thomas Hood
from *The Two Swans*

And bright and silvery the willows sleep
Over the shady verge – no mad winds tease
Their hoary heads; but quietly they weep
Their sprinkling leaves – half fountains and half trees:
There lilies be – and fairer than all these,
A solitary Swan her breast of snow
Launches against the wave that seems to freeze
Into a chaste reflection, still below,
Twin-shadow of herself wherever she may go.

DUCKS' DITTY

by Kenneth Grahame

All along the backwater,
Through the rushes tall,
Ducks are a-dabbling.
Up tails all!

Ducks' tails, drakes' tails,
Yellow feet a-quiver,
Yellow bills all out of sight
Busy in the river!

Slushy green undergrowth
Where the roach swim –
Here we keep our larder,
Cool and full and dim.

Every one for what he likes!
We like to be
Heads down, tails up,
Dabbling free!

High in the blue above
Swifts whirl and call –
We are down a-dabbling
Up tails all!

THE PIKE

by Edmund Blunden

From shadows of rich oaks outpeer
The moss-green bastions of the weir,
Where the quick dipper forages
In elver-peopled crevices,
And a small runlet trickling down the sluice
Gossamer music tires not to unloose.

Else round the broad pool's hush
    Nothing stirs,
Unless sometimes a straggling heifer crush
Through the thronged spinney where the pheasant whirs;
    Or martins in a flash
Come with wild mirth to dip their magical wings,
While in the shallow some doomed bulrush swings
At whose hid root the diver vole's teeth gnash.

And nigh this toppling reed, still as the dead
    The great pike lies, the murderous patriarch
    Watching the waterpit sheer-shelving dark,
Where through the plash his lithe bright vassals thread.

The rose-finned roach and bluish bream
And staring ruffe steal up the stream
Hard by their glutted tyrant, now
Still as a sunken bough.

He on the sandbank lies,
  Sunning himself long hours
With stony gorgon eyes:
  Westward the hot sun lowers.

Sudden the gray pike changes, and quivering poises for
  slaughter;
  Intense terror wakens around him, the shoals scud awry,
    but there chances
  A chub unsuspecting; the prowling fins quicken, in
    fury he lances;
And the miller that opens the hatch stands amazed at the
  whirl in the water.

ON THIS ISLAND

by W.H. Auden

Look, stranger, on this island now
The leaping light for your delight discovers,
Stand stable here
And silent be,
That through the channels of the ear
May wander like a river
The swaying sound of the sea.

Here at a small field's ending pause
Where the chalk wall falls to the foam and its tall ledges
Oppose the pluck
And knock of the tide,
And the shingle scrambles after the suck-
-ing surf, and a gull lodges
A moment on its sheer side.

Far off like floating seeds the ships
Diverge on urgent voluntary errands;
And this full view
Indeed may enter
And move in memory as now these clouds do,
That pass the harbour mirror
And all the summer through the water saunter.

'WITH A SWIMMER'S STROKE'

by George Gordon, Lord Byron
from The Two Foscari
(act 1, scene 1)

How many a time have I
Cloven with arms still lustier, breast more daring,
The wave all roughened; with a swimmer's stroke
Flinging the billows back from my drench'd hair,
And laughing from my lip the audacious brine,
Which kiss'd it like a wine-cup, rising o'er
The waves as they arose, and prouder still
The loftier they uplifted me; and oft,
In wantonness of spirit, plunging down
Into their green and glassy gulfs, and making
My way to shells and sea-weed, all unseen
By those above, till they waxed fearful; then
Returning with my grasp full of such tokens
As showed that I had searched the deep: exulting,
With a far-dashing stroke, and drawing deep
The long-suspended breath, again I spurned
The foam which broke around me, and pursued
My track like a sea-bird.

SEA-WEED

by D.H. Lawrence

Sea-weed sways and sways and swirls
as if swaying were its form of stillness;
and if it flushes against fierce rock
it slips over it as shadows do, without hurting itself.

THE DEAD CRAB

by Andrew Young

A rosy shield upon its back,
That not the hardest storm could crack,
From whose sharp edge projected out
Black pinpoint eyes staring about;
Beneath, the well-knit cote-armure
That gave to its weak belly power;
The clustered legs with plated joints
That ended in stiletto points;
The claws like mouths it held outside:
I cannot think this creature died
By storm or fish or sea-fowl harmed
Walking the sea so heavily armed;
Or does it make for death to be
Oneself a living armoury?

HAREBELLS OVER MANNIN BAY

by C. Day Lewis

Half moon of moon-pale sand.
Sea stirs in midnight blue.
Looking across to the Twelve Pins
The singular harebells stand.

The sky's all azure. Eye
To eye with them upon
Cropped grass, I note the harebells give
Faint echoes of the sky.

For such a Lilliput host
To pit their colours against
Peacock of sea and mountain seems
Impertinence at least.

These summer commonplaces,
Seen close enough, confound
A league of brilliant waves, and dance
On the grave mountain faces.

Harebells, keep your arresting
Pose by the strand. I like
These gestures of the ephemeral
Against the everlasting.

LONG LION DAYS

by Philip Larkin

Long lion days
Start with white haze.
By midday you meet
A hammer of heat –
Whatever was sown
Now fully grown,
Whatever conceived
Now fully leaved,
Abounding, ablaze –
O long lion days!

'OH WHAT UNUSUAL HEATS ARE HERE'

by Andrew Marvell
from *Damon the Mower*

Oh what unusual Heats are here,
Which thus our Sun-burn'd Meadows sear!
The Grass-hopper its pipe gives ore;
And hamstring'd Frogs can dance no more.
But in the brook the green Frog wades;
And Grass-hoppers seek out the shades.
Only the Snake, that kept within,
Now glitters in its second skin.

from THE GRASSHOPPER

by Richard Lovelace

O thou that swings't upon the waving hair
  Of some well-filled oaten beard,
Drunk every night with a delicious tear
  Dropt thee from heaven, where th'art rear'd!

The joys of earth and air are thine entire,
  That with thy feet and wings dost hop and fly;
And when thy poppy works, thou dost retire
  To thy carved acorn-bed to lie.

Up with the day, the Sun thou welcom'st then,
Sport'st in the gilt plaits of his beams,
And all these merry days mak'st merry men,
Thyself, and melancholy streams.

AUGUST

by Andrew Young

The cows stood in a thundercloud of flies,
  As lagging though the field with trailing feet
I kicked up scores of skipper butterflies
  That hopped a little way, lazy with heat.

The wood I found was in deep shelter sunk,
  Though bryony leaves shone with a glossy sweat
And creeping over ground and up tree-trunk
  The ivy in the sun gleamed bright and wet.

Songs brief as Chinese poems the birds sung
  And insects of all sheens, blue, brown and yellow,
Darted and twisted in their flight and hung
  On air that groaned like hoarse sweet violoncello.

No leaf stirred in the wood-discouraged wind,
  But foliage hung on trees, like heavy wigs;
The sun, come from the sky, was close behind
  The fire-fringed leaves and in among the twigs.

from A RUNNABLE STAG

by John Davidson

When the pods went pop on the broom, green broom,
And the apples began to be golden-skinned,
We harboured a stag in the Priory coomb,
And we feathered his trail up-wind, up-wind,
We feathered his trail up-wind –
A stag of warrant, a stag, a stag,
A runnable stag, a kingly crop,
Brow, bay and tray and three on top,
A stag, a runnable stag.

Then the huntsman's horn rang yap, yap yap,
And 'Forwards' we heard the harbourer shout;
But 'twas only a brocket that broke a gap
In the beechen underwood, driven out,
From the underwood antlered out
By warrant and might of the stag, the stag,
The runnable stag, whose lordly mind
Was bent on sleep, though beamed and tined
He stood, a runnable stag.

So we tufted the covert till afternoon
With Tinkerman's Pup and Bell-of-the-North;
And hunters were sulky and hounds out of tune
Before we tufted the right stag forth,
Before we tufted him forth,
The stag of warrant, the wily stag,
The runnable stag with his kingly crop,
Brow, bay and tray and three on top,
The royal and runnable stag.

It was Bell-of-the-North and Tinkerman's Pup
That stuck to the scent till the copse was drawn.
'Tally ho! tally ho!' and the hunt was up,
The tufters whipped and the pack laid on,
The resolute pack laid on,
And the stag of warrant away at last,
The runnable stag, the same, the same,
His hoofs on fire, his horns like flame,
A stag, a runnable stag.

. . . .

For a matter of twenty miles and more,
By the densest hedge and the highest wall,
Through herds of bullocks he baffled the lore
Of harbourer, huntsman, hounds and all,
Of harbourer hounds and all —
The stag of warrant, the wily stag,
For twenty miles, and five and five,
He ran, and he never was caught alive,
This stag, this runnable stag.

When he turned at bay in the leafy gloom,
In the emerald gloom where the brook ran deep,
He heard in the distance the rollers boom,
And he saw in a vision of peaceful sleep,
In a wonderful vision of sleep,
A stag of warrant, a stag, a stag,
A runnable stag in a jewelled bed
Under the sheltering ocean dead,
A stag, a runnable stag.

So a fateful hope lit up his eye,
And he opened his nostrils wide again,
And he tossed his branching antlers high
As he headed the hunt down the Charlock glen,
As he raced down the echoing glen –
For five miles more, the stag, the stag,
For twenty miles, and five and five,
Not to be caught now, dead or alive,
The stag, the runnable stag.

Three hundred gentlemen, able to ride,
Three hundred horses as gallant and free,
Beheld him escape on the evening tide,
Far out till he sank in the Severn Sea,
Till he sank in the depths of the sea –
The stag, the buoyant stag, the stag
That slept at last in a jewelled bed
Under the sheltering ocean spread,
The stag, the runnable stag.

DAY-DREAMS

by William Canton

Broad August burns in milky skies,
　　The world is blanched with hazy heat;
The vast green pasture, even, lies
　　Too hot and bright for eyes and feet.

Amid the grassy levels rears
　　The sycamore against the sun
The dark boughs of a hundred years,
　　The emerald foliage of one.

Lulled in a dream of shade and sheen,
　　Within the clement twilight thrown
By that great cloud of floating green,
　　A horse is standing, still as stone.

He stirs nor head nor hoof, although
　　The grass is fresh beneath the branch;
His tail alone swings to and fro
　　In graceful curves from haunch to haunch.

He stands quite lost, indifferent
　　To rack or pasture, trace or rein;
He feels the vaguely sweet content
　　Of perfect sloth in limb and brain.

HIGH SUMMER

by Ebenezer Jones

I never wholly feel that summer is high,
However green the trees, or loud the birds,
However movelessly eye-winking herds
Stand in field ponds, or under large trees lie,
Till I do climb all cultured pastures by,
That hedged by hedgerows studiously fretted trim,
Smile like a lady's face with lace laced prim,
And on some moor or hill that seeks the sky
Lonely and nakedly, – utterly lie down,
And feel the sunshine throbbing on body and limb,
My drowsy brain in pleasant drunkenness swim,
Each rising thought sink back and dreamily drown,
Smiles creep o'er my face, and smother my lips, and cloy,
Each muscle sink to itself, and separately enjoy.

WINDY DAY IN AUGUST

by C. Day Lewis

Over the vale, the sunburnt fields
A wind from the sea like as streamer unreels:
Dust leaps up, apples thud down,
The river's caught between a smile and a frown.

An inn-sign swinging, swinging to the wind,
Whines and whinges like a dog confined,
Round his paddock gallops the colt,
Dinghies at moorings curvet and jolt.

Sunlight and shadow in the copse play tig,
While the wallowing clouds talk big
About their travels, and thistledown blows
Ghosting above the rank hedgerows.

Cornfield, orchard and fernland hail
Each other, waving from hill to hill:
They change their colours from morn to night
In play with the lissom, engaging light.

The wind roars endlessly past my ears,
Racing my heart as in earlier years.
Here and everywhere, then and now
Earth moves like a wanton, breathes like a vow.

SUMMER RAIN

by Hartley Coleridge

Thick lay the dust, uncomfortably white,
In glaring mimicry of Arab sand.
The woods and mountains slept in hazy light;
The meadows look'd athirst and tawny tanned;
The little rills had left their channels bare,
With scarce a pool to witness what they were;
And the shrunk river gleamed 'mid oozy stones,
That stared like any famished giant's bones.
Sudden the hills grew black, and hot as stove
The air beneath; it was a toil to be.
There was a growling as of angry Jove,
Provoked by Juno's prying jealousy –
A flash – a crash – the firmament was split,
And down it came in drops – the smallest fit
To drown a bee in fox-glove bell conceal'd;
Joy filled the brook, and comfort cheered the field.

from **ON THE UNUSUAL COLD AND RAINIE WEATHER IN THE SUMMER, 1648**

by Robert Heath

Why puts our Grandame Nature on
Her winter coat, ere Summer's done?
What, hath she got an ague fit?
And thinks to make us hov'ring sit
Over her lazie embers? Else why should
Old Hyems freeze our vernal blood?
Or as we each day, grow older,
Doth the world wax wan and colder?

THE RAINY SUMMER

by Alice Meynell

There's much afoot in heaven and earth this year;
   The winds hunt up the sun, hunt up the moon,
Trouble the dubious dawn, hasten the drear
   Height of a threatening noon.

No breath of boughs, no breath of leaves, of fronds,
   May linger or grow warm; the trees are loud;
The forest, rooted, tosses in her bonds,
   And strains against the cloud.

No scents may pause within the garden-fold;
   The rifled flowers are cold as ocean-shells;
Bees, humming in the storm, carry their cold
   Wild honey to cold cells.

'FOR SO WORK THE HONEY BEES'

by William Shakespeare
from *Henry V*
(act 1, scene 2)

For so work the honey bees;
Creatures that, by rule in nature, teach
The act of order to a peopled kingdom.
They have a king, and officers of sorts:
Which some, like merchants, venture trade abroad;
Others, like soldiers, armed in their stings,
Make boot upon the summer's velvet buds;
Which pillage they with merry march bring home
To the tent-royal of their emperor:
Who, busied in his majesty, surveys
The singing masons bringing roofs of gold;
The civil citizens kneading up the honey;
The poor mechanic porters crowding in
Their heavy burdens at his narrow gate;
The sad-ey'd justice, with his surly hum,
Delivering over to executors pale
The lazy yawning drone.

THE RAINBOW

by Walter de la Mare

I saw the lovely arch
of Rainbow span the sky,
The gold sun burning
As the rain swept by.

In bright-ringed solitude
The showery foliage shone
One lovely moment,
And the Bow was gone.

HAYMAKING

by Edward Thomas

After night's thunder far away had rolled
The fiery day had a kernel sweet of cold,
And in the perfect blue the clouds uncurled,
Like the first gods before they made the world
And misery, swimming the stormless sea
In beauty and in divine gaiety.
The smooth white empty road was lightly strewn
With leaves – the holly's Autumn falls in June –
And fir cones standing stiff up in the heat.
The mill-foot water tumbled white and lit
With tossing crystals, happier than any crowd
Of children pouring out of school aloud.
And in the little thickets where a sleeper
For ever might lie lost, the nettle-creeper
And garden warbler sang unceasingly;
While over them shrill shrieked in his fierce glee
The swift with wings and tail as sharp and narrow
As if the bow had flown off with the arrow.
Only the scent of woodbine and hay new-mown
Travelled the road. In the field sloping down,
Park-like, to where its willows showed the brook,
Haymakers rested. The tosser lay forsook
Out in the sun; and the long waggon stood
Without its team; it seemed it never would
Move from the shadow of that single yew.
The team, as still, until their task was due,
Beside the labourers enjoyed the shade
That three squat oaks mid-field together made

Upon a circle of grass and weed uncut,
And on the hollow, once a chalk-pit, but
Now brimmed with nut and elder-flower so clean.
The men leaned on their rakes, about to begin,
But still. And all were silent. All was old,
This morning time, with a great age untold,
Older than Clare and Cowper, Morland and Crome,
Than, at the field's far edge, the farmer's home,
A white house crouched at the foot of a great tree.
Under the heavens that know not what years be
The men, the beasts, the trees, the implements
Uttered even what they will in times far hence –
All of us gone out of the reach of change –
Immortal in a picture of an old grange.

BOTH HARVESTS

by Ken Smith

Guns twitch the gloved ears of the rabbit,
that ripened with the corn. Summer
was burrowed, with the young peering
over green shoots. Now they move
under red corn. But blades are set
and honed. A tractor roves the scythed
edges. These men who stook and bend,
bend and stook, have their business
with grain. Those who come after,
come to kill, gun under shoulder.
A rabbit is a grey thing running,
stopped, hung in air, dead. Some
hide under bound sheaves. Some panic
into the mower and are savaged, blood,
bone, and pelt. Set blades are determined.
Rabbits die running, not like standing grain
cut clean. The field is clear, its straw
lined and ordered: it will be bread
and bedding for safe cattle. The rabbit
need not fear the winter. Shot corpses
brace under fur, are shared out evenly.

BLACKBERRY-PICKING

by Seamus Heaney

Late August, given heavy rain and sun
For a full week, the blackberries would ripen.
At first, just one, a glossy purple clot
Among others, red, green, hard as a knot.
You ate that first one and its flesh was sweet
Like thickened wine: summer's blood was in it
Leaving stains upon the tongue and lust for
Picking. Then red ones inked up, and that hunger
Sent us out with milk-cans, pea-tins, jam-pots
Where briars scratched and wet grass bleached our boots.
Round hayfields, cornfields and potato-drills,
We trekked and picked until the cans were full,
Until the tinkling bottom had been covered
With green ones, and on top big dark blobs burned
Like a plate of eyes. Our hands were peppered
With thorn pricks, our palms sticky as Bluebeard's.

We hoarded the fresh berries in the byre.
But when the bath was filled we found a fur,
A rat-grey fungus, glutting on our cache.
The juice was stinking too. Once off the bush,
The fruit fermented, the sweet flesh would turn sour.
I always felt like crying. It wasn't fair
That all the lovely canfuls smelt of rot.
Each year I hoped they'd keep, knew they would not.

'WHAT WONDROUS LIFE IS THIS I LEAD'

by Andrew Marvell
from Thoughts in a Garden

What wondrous life is this I lead!
Ripe apples drop about my head;
The luscious clusters of the vine
Upon my mouth do crush their wine.
The nectarine and curious peach,
Into my hands themselves do reach;
Stumbling on melons, as I pass,
Ensnared with flowers, I fall on grass.

102

APPLES

by Laurie Lee

Behold the apples' rounded worlds:
juice-green of July rain,
the black polestar of flower, the rind
mapped with its crimson stain.

The russet, crab and cottage red
burn to the sun's hot brass,
then drop like sweat from every branch
and bubble in the grass.

They lie as wanton as they fall,
and where they fall and break,
the stallion clamps his crunching jaws,
the starling stabs his beak.

In each plump gourd the cidery bite
of boys' teeth tears the skin;
the waltzing wasp consumes his share,
the bent worm enters in.

I, with as easy hunger, take
entire my season's dole;
welcome the ripe, the sweet, the sour,
the hollow and the whole.

THISTLES

by Ted Hughes

Against the rubber tongues of cows and the hoeing hands of men
Thistles spike the summer air
And crackle open under a blue-black pressure.

Every one a revengeful burst
Of resurrection, a grasped fistful
Of splintered weapons and Icelandic frost thrust up

From the underground stain of a decayed Viking.
They are like pale hair and the gutturals of dialects.
Every one manages a plume of blood.

Then they grow, like men.
Mown down, it is a feud. Their sons appear,
Stiff with weapons, fighting back over the same ground.

CUT GRASS

by Philip Larkin

Cut grass lies frail:
Brief is the breath
Mown stalks exhale.
Long, long the death

It dies in the white hours
Of young-leafed June
With chestnut flowers,
With hedges snowlike strewn,

White lilac bowed,
Lost lanes of Queen Anne's lace,
And that high-builded cloud
Moving at summer's pace.

MOUSE'S NEST

by John Clare

I found a ball of grass among the hay
And progged it as I passed and went away;
And when I looked I fancied something stirred,
And turned agen and hoped to catch the bird –
When out an old mouse bolted in the wheats
With all her young ones hanging at her teats;
She looked so odd and so grotesque to me,
I ran and wondered what the thing could be,
And pushed the knapweed bunches where I stood;
Then the mouse hurried from the craking brood.
The young ones squeaked, and as I went away
She found her nest again among the hay.
The water o'er the pebbles scarce could run
And broad old cesspools glittered in the sun.

THE SUBLIME

by Wilfrid Scawen Blunt
from The Love Sonnets of Proteus
(Part IV: Vita Nova)

To stand upon a windy pinnacle,
Beneath the infinite blue of the blue noon,
And underfoot a valley terrible
As that dim gulf, where sense and being swoon
When the soul parts; a giant valley strewn
With giant rocks; asleep, and vast, and still,
And far away. The torrent, which has hewn
His pathway through the entrails of the hill,
Now crawls along the bottom and anon
Lifts up his voice, a muffled tremulous roar,
Borne on the wind an instant, and then gone
Back to the caverns of the middle air;
A voice as of a nation overthrown
With beat of drums, when hosts have marched to war.

RANNOCH, BY GLENCOE

by T.S. Eliot

Here the crow starves, here the patient stag
Breeds for the rifle. Between the soft moor
And the soft sky, scarcely room
To leap or soar. Substance crumbles, in the thin air
Moon cold or moon hot. The road winds in
Listlessness of ancient war,
Languor of broken steel,
Clamour of confused wrong, apt
In silence. Memory is strong
Beyond the bone. Pride snapped,
Shadow of pride is long, in the long pass
No concurrence of bone.

THE ELVERS

by Norman Nicholson

An iron pipe
Syphoning gallons of brine
From the hundred foot below sea-level mine –
A spring salty as mussels,
Bilberry-stained with ore;
And the pink, dry-paper thrift rustles
In the draught made by the spray
As the pumps thrust the water upward
To a rock-locked bay.

And, quick in the brown burn,
Black whips that flick and shake,
Live darning-needles with big-eye heads –
Five-inch elvers
That for twice five seasons snake
Through the earth's turn and return of water
To seep with the swell into rifts of the old workings
And be churned out here on cinder beds and fern.

The pumps pour on.
The elvers shimmy in the weed. And I,
Beneath my parochial complement of sky,
Plot their way
From Sargasso Sea to Cumberland,
From tide to pit,
Knowing the why of it
No more than they.

HEATHER

---

by Eifion Wyn

They grow so comely, a quiet host, fine gems
   Of the shire of sun and breeze,
   Bells hanging from high rock places,
   Flowers of the stone, phials of honey.

Translated from the Welsh
by Tony Conran

THE EAGLE

---

by Alfred, Lord Tennyson

He clasps the crag with crooked hands;
Close to the sun in lonely lands,
Ring'd with the azure world, he stands.

The wrinkled sea beneath him crawls;
He watches from his mountain walls,
And like a thunderbolt he falls.

THE HERMIT'S SONG

Anonymous (7th century)

A hiding tuft, a green-barked yew tree
Is my roof,
While nearby a great oak keeps me
Tempest-proof.

A clear well beside me offers
Best of drink,
And there grows a bed of cresses
Near its brink.

Pigs and goats, the friendliest neighbours,
Nestle near,
Wild swine come, or broods of badgers,
Grazing deer.

All the gentry of the country
Come to call!
And the foxes come behind them,
Best of all.

To what meals the woods invite me
All about!
There are water, herbs and cresses,
Salmon, trout.

A clutch of eggs, sweet mast and honey
Are my meat,
Heathberries and whortleberries
For a sweet.

All that one could ask for comfort
Round me grows,
There are hips and haws and strawberries,
Nuts and sloes.

And when summer spreads its mantle
What a sight!
Marjoram and leeks and pignuts,
Juicy, bright.

Dainty redbreasts briskly forage
Every bush,
Round and round there flutter
Swallow, thrush.

Bees and beetles, music-makers,
Croon and strum;
Geese pass over, duck in autumn
Dark streams hum.

Angry wren, officious linnet
And black-cap,
All industrious, and the woodpecker's
Sturdy tap.

From the sea the gulls and herons
Flutter in,
While in upland heather rises
The grey hen.

In the year's most brilliant weather
Heifers low
Through green fields, not driven nor beaten,
Tranquil, slow.

In wreathed boughs the wind is whispering,
Skies are blue,
Swans call, river water falling
Is calling too.

Translated from the Irish
by Frank O'Connor

DREAM-FOREST

by Siegfried Sassoon

Where sunshine flecks the green,
Through towering woods my way
Goes winding all the day.

Scant are the flowers that bloom
Beneath the bosky screen
And cage of golden gloom.
Few are the birds that call,
Shrill-voiced and seldom seen.

Where silence masters all,
And light my footsteps fall,
The whispering runnels only
With blazing noon confer;
And comes no breeze to stir
The tangled thickets lonely.

THE DARK WOOD

by Andrew Young

O wood, now you are dark with summer
Your birds grow dumber
And ink-stained leaves of sycamore
Slide slowly down and hit your floor;
But there are other signs I mark,
In ivy with the sunlight wet
And dried rains streaming down your bark,
A withered limb, a broken shoulder,
Signs that since first we met
Even you, O wood, have grown a little older.

THE COMBE

by Edward Thomas

The Combe was ever dark, ancient and dark.
Its mouth is stopped with bramble, thorn and briar;
And no one scrambles over the sliding chalk
By beech and yew and perishing juniper
Down the half precipices of its sides, with roots
And rabbit holes for steps. The sun of Winter,
The moon of Summer, and all the singing birds
Except the missel-thrush that loves juniper,
Are quite shut out. But far more ancient and dark
The Combe looks since they killed the badger there,
Dug him out and gave him to the hounds,
That most ancient Briton of English beasts.

THE WAY THROUGH THE WOODS

by Rudyard Kipling

They shut the road through the woods
Seventy years ago.
Weather and rain have undone it again,
And now you would never know
There was once a road through the woods
Before they planted the trees.
It is underneath the coppice and heath
And the thin anemones.
Only the keeper sees
That, where the ring-dove broods,
And the badgers roll at ease,
There was once a road through the woods.

Yet, if you enter the woods
Of a summer evening late,
When the night-air cools on the trout-ringed pools
Where otter whistles his mate,
(They fear not men in the woods,
Because they see so few)
You will hear the beat of a horse's feet,
And the swish of a skirt in the dew,
Steadily cantering through
The misty solitudes,
As though they perfectly knew
The old lost road through the woods . . .
But there is no road through the woods.

Among the Firs

by Eugene Lee-Hamilton

And what a charm is in the rich hot scent
  Of old fir heated by the sun,
  Where drops of resin down the rough bark run,
And needle litter breathes its wonderment.

The old fir forests heated by the sun,
  Their thought shall linger like the lingering scent,
  Their beauty haunt us, and a wonderment
Of moss, of fern, of cones, of rills that run.

The needle litter breathes a wonderment;
  The crimson crans are sparkling in the sun;
  From tree to tree the scampering squirrels run;
The hum of insects blends with heat and scent.

The drops of resin down the rough bark run;
  And riper, ever riper, grows the scent;
  But eve has come, to end the wonderment,
And slowly up the tree trunk climbs the sun.

from THE NATURALIST'S SUMMER-EVENING WALK

by Gilbert White

To Thomas Pennant, Esq

When the day declining sheds a milder gleam,
What time the may-fly haunts the pool or stream;
When the still owl skims round the grassy mead,
What time the timorous hare limps forth to feed;
Then be the time to steal adown the vale,
And listen to the vagrant cuckoo's tale;
To hear the clamorous curlew call his mate,
Or the soft quail his tender pain relate;
To see the swallow sweep the dark'ning plain
Belated, to support her infant train;
To mark the swift in rapid giddy ring
Dash round the steeple, unsubdued of wing:
Amusive birds! – say where your hid retreat
When the frost rages and the tempests beat;
Whence your return, by such nice instinct led,
When spring, soft season, lifts her bloomy head?
Such baffled searches mock a man's prying pride,
The God of Nature is your secret guide!
　While deep'ning shades obscure the face of day,
To yonder bench, leaf-sheltered, let us stray,
Till blended objects fail the swimming sight,
And all the fading landscape sinks in night;
To hear the drowsy dor come brushing by
With buzzing wing, or the shrill cricket cry;
To see the feeding bat glance through the wood;
To catch the distant falling of the flood;

119

While o'er the cliff th'awakened churn-owl hung
Through the still gloom protracts his chattering song;
While high in air, and poised upon his wings,
Unseen, the soft, enamoured woodlark sings:
These, Nature's works, the curious mind employ,
Inspire a soothing melancholy joy . . .

from THE BUZZARDS

by Martin Armstrong

When evening came and the warm glow grew deeper,
And every tree that bordered the green meadows,
And in the yellow cornfields every reaper
And every corn-shock stood above their shadows
Flung eastward from their feet in longer measure,
Serenely far there swam in the sunny height
A buzzard and his mate who took their pleasure
Swirling and poising idly in golden light.
On great pied motionless moth-wings borne along,
   So effortless and so strong,
Cutting each other's paths, together they glided,
Then wheeled asunder till they soared divided
Two valleys' width (as though it were delight
To part like this, being sure they could unite
So swiftly in their empty, free dominion),
Curved headlong downward, towered up the sunny steep,
Then with sudden lift of the one great pinion,
Swung proudly to a curve, and from its height
Took half a mile of sunlight in one long sweep.

HARES AT PLAY

by John Clare

The birds are gone to bed the cows are still
And sheep lie panting on each old mole hill
And underneath the willows grey-green bough
Like toil a resting – lies the fallow plough
The timid hares throw daylights fears away
On the lanes road to dust and dance and play
Then dabble in the grain by nought deterred
To lick the dewfall from the barleys beard
Then out they sturt again and round the hill
Like happy thoughts dance squat and loiter still
Till milking maidens in the early morn
Gingle their yokes and start them in the corn
Through well known beaten paths each nimbling hare
Sturts quick as fear – and seeks its hidden lair

ENGLAND

by Edith Nesbit

Shoulders of upland brown laid dark to the sunset's bosom,
　Living amber of wheat, and copper of new-ploughed loam,
Downs where the white sheep wander, little gardens in
　　blossom,
　Roads that wind through the twilight up to the lights of home.
Lanes that are white with hawthorn, dykes where the sedges
　　shiver,
　Hollows where caged winds slumber, moorlands where winds
　　wake free,
Sowing and reaping and gleaning, spring and torrent and river,
　Are they not more, by worlds, than the whole of the world
　　can be?
Is there a corner of land, a furze-fringed rag of a by-way
　Coign of your foam-white cliffs or swirl of your grass-green
　　waves,
Leaf of your peaceful copse, or dust of your strenuous highway,
　But in our hearts is sacred, dear as our cradles, our graves?
Is not each bough in your orchards, each cloud in the skies
　　above you,
　Is not each byre or homestead, furrow or farm or fold,
Dear as the last dear drops of the blood in the hearts that love
　　you,
　Filling those hearts till the love is more than the heart can
　　hold?

THE HARVEST MOON

by Ted Hughes

The flame-red moon, the harvest moon,
Rolls along the hills, gently bouncing,
A vast balloon,
Till it takes off, and sinks upward
To lie in the bottom of the sky, like a gold doubloon.

The harvest moon has come,
Booming softly through heaven, like a bassoon.
And earth replies all night, like a deep drum.

So people can't sleep,
So they go out where elms and oak trees keep
A kneeling vigil, in a religious hush.
The harvest moon has come!

And all the moonlit cows and all the sheep
Stare up at her petrified, while she swells
Filling heaven, as if red hot, and sailing
Closer and closer like the end of the world.

Till the gold fields of stiff wheat
Cry 'We are ripe, reap us!' and the rivers
Sweat from the melting hills.

'I KNOW A GROVE'

by Samuel Taylor Coleridge
from The Nightingale

I know a grove
Of large extent, hard by a castle huge,
Which the great lord inhabits not; and so
This grove is wild with tangling underwood,
And the trim walks are broken up, and grass,
Thin grass and king-cups grow within the paths.
But never elsewhere in one place I knew
So many nightingales; and far and near
In wood and thicket, over the wide grove,
They answer and provoke each other's song,
With skirmish and capricious passagings,
And murmurs musical and swift jug jug,
And one low piping sound more sweet than all
Stirring the air with such a harmony,
That should you close your eyes, you might almost
Forget it was not day! On moonlit bushes
Whose dewy leaflets are but half-disclosed,
You may perchance behold them on the twigs,
Their bright, bright eyes, their eyes both bright and full,
Glistening, while many a glow-worm in the shade
Lights up her love-torch.

JASMINE

by Thomas Moore

Plants that wake when other sleep –
Timid jasmine buds that keep
Their fragrance to themselves all day,
But when the sunlight dies away
Let the delicious secret out
To every breeze that roams about.

'AH GOD! TO SEE THE BRANCHES STIR'

by Rupert Brooke
from *The Old Vicarage, Grantchester*

Ah God! to see the branches stir
Across the moon at Grantchester!
To smell the thrilling-sweet and rotten,
Unforgettable, unforgotten
River-smell, and hear the breeze
Sobbing in the little trees.
Say, do the elm-clumps greatly stand,
Still guardians of that holy land?
The chestnuts shade, in reverend dream,
The yet unacademic stream?
Is dawn a secret shy and cold
Anadyomene, silver-gold?
And sunset still a golden sea
From Haslingfield to Madingley?
And after, ere the night is born,
Do hares come out about the corn?
Oh, is the water sweet and cool
Gentle and brown, above the pool?
And laughs the immortal river still
Under the mill, under the mill?
Say, is there Beauty yet to find?
And Certainty? and Quiet kind?
Deep meadows yet, for to forget
The lies, and truths, and pain? . . . Oh! yet
Stands the Church clock at ten to three?
And is there honey still for tea?

127

SWEET SUFFOLK OWL

by Thomas Vautor

Sweet Suffolk owl, so trimly dight
With feathers like a lady bright,
Thou singest alone, sitting by night,
Te whit, te whoo, te whit, te whit.
Thy note, that forth so freely rolls,
With shrill command the mouse controls,
And sings a dirge for dying souls,
Te whit, te whoo, te whit, te whit.

TO THE EVENING STAR

by William Blake

Thou fair-haired angel of the evening,
Now, whilst the sun rests in the mountains, light
Thy bright torch of love; thy radiant crown
Put on, and smile upon our evening bed!
Smile on our loves; and, while thou drawest the
Blue curtains of the sky, scatter thy silver dew
On every flower that shuts its sweet eyes
In timely sleep. Let thy west wind sleep on
The lake; speak silence with thy glimmering eyes,
And wash the dusk with silver. Soon, full soon,
Dost thou withdraw; then the wolf rages wide,
And the lion glares through the dun forest.
The fleeces of our flocks are covered with
Thy sacred dew: protect them with thine influence.

'MIDNIGHT WAS COME, WHEN EVERY VITAL THING'

by Thomas Sackville, Lord Buckhurst
from *Midnight*

Midnight was come, when every vital thing
With sweet sound sleep their weary limbs did rest,
The beasts were still, the little birds that sing
Now sweetly slept, beside their mother's breast,
The old and all were shrouded in their nest:
   The waters calm, the cruel seas did cease,
   The woods, and fields, and all things held their peace.

The golden stars were whirled amid their race,
And on the earth did laugh with twinkling light,
When each thing, nestled in his resting-place,
Forgat day's pain with pleasure of the night:
The hare had not the greedy hounds in sight,
   The fearful deer of death stood not in doubt,
   The partridge dreamed not of the falcon's foot.

THERE CAME A DAY

by Ted Hughes

There came a day that caught the summer
Wrung its neck
Plucked it
And ate it.

Now what shall I do with the trees?
The day said, the day said.
Strip them bare, strip them bare.
Let's see what is really there.

And what shall I do with the sun?
The day said, the day said.
Roll him away till he's cold and small.
He'll come back rested if he comes back at all.

And what shall I do with the birds?
The day said, the day said.
The birds I've frightened, let them flit,
I'll hang out pork for the brave tomtit.

And what shall I do with the seed?
The day said, the day said.
Bury it deep, see what it's worth.
See if it can stand the earth.

What shall I do with the people?
The day said, the day said.
Stuff them with apple and blackberry pie –
They'll love me then till the day they die.

There came this day and he was autumn.
His mouth was wide
And red as a sunset.
His tail was an icicle.

AUTUMN

Now every day the bracken browner grows,
Even the purple stars
Of clematis, that shone about the bars,
Grow browner; and the little autumn rose
Dons, for her rosy gown,
Sad weeds of brown.

from *September*
Mary Coleridge

DAY HAD AWAKENED

by Percy Bysshe Shelley

Day had awakened all things that be,
   The lark and the thrush and the swallow free,
  And the milkmaid's song and the mower's scythe,
And the matin-bell and the mountain bee:
Fireflies were quenched on the dewy corn,
   Glow-worms went out on the river's brim,
   Like lamps which a student forgets to trim:
The beetle forgot to wind his horn,
   The crickets were still in the meadow and hill:
Like a flock of rooks at a farmer's gun
Night's dreams and terrors, every one,
Fled from the brains which are their prey
From the lamp's death to the morning ray.

TO AUTUMN

by John Keats

Season of mists and mellow fruitfulness,
Close bosom-friend of the maturing sun;
Conspiring with him how to load and bless
With fruit the vines that round the thatch-eaves run;
To bend with apples the moss'd cottage-trees,
And fill all fruit with ripeness to the core;
To swell the gourd, and plump the hazel shells
With a sweet kernel; to set budding more,
And still more, later flowers for the bees,
Until they think warm days will never cease,
For Summer has o'er-brimm'd their clammy cells.

Who hath not seen thee oft amid thy store?
Sometimes whoever seeks abroad may find
Thee sitting careless on a granary floor,
Thy hair soft-lifted by the winnowing wind;
Or on a half-reap'd furrow sound asleep,
Drows'd with the fume of poppies, while thy hook
Spares the next swath and all its twined flowers:
And sometimes like a gleaner thou dost keep
Steady thy laden head across a brook;
Or by a cider-press, with patient look,
Thou watchest the last oozings, hours by hours.

Where are the songs of Spring? Ay, where are they?
Think not of them, thou hast thy music too —
While barred clouds bloom the soft-dying day,
And touch the stubble-plains with rosy hue;
Then in a wailful choir, the small gnats mourn
Among the river sallows, borne aloft
Or sinking as the light wind lives or dies;
And full-grown lambs loud bleat from hilly bourn;
Hedge-crickets sing; and now with treble soft
The redbreast whistles from a garden-croft,
And gathering swallows twitter in the skies.

from **THE DEPARTURE OF SUMMER**

by Thomas Hood

Summer is gone on swallows' wings,
And Earth has buried all her flowers:
No more the lark, the linnet sings,
But Silence sits in faded bowers.
There is a shadow on the plain
Of Winter ere he comes again, –
There is in woods a solemn sound
Of hollow warnings whispered round,
As Echo in her deep recess
For once had turned a prophetess.
Shuddering Autumn stops to list,
And breathes his fear in sudden sighs,
With clouded face, and hazel eyes
That quench themselves, and hide in mist.

'THEN CAME THE AUTUMN ALL IN YELLOW CLAD'

by Edmund Spenser
from *The Faerie Queen*
(Book VII, canto VII, stanza 30)

Then came the Autumn all in yellow clad,
As though he joyed in his plenteous store,
Laden with fruits that made him laugh, full glad,
That he had banished hunger, which to-fore
Had by the belly oft him pinchèd sore.
Upon his head a wreath, that was enrolled
With ears of corn of every sort, he bore;
And in his hand a sickle he did hold,
To reap the ripened fruits the which the earth had yold.

THE GARDEN IN SEPTEMBER

by Robert Bridges

Now thin mists temper the slow-ripening beams
Of the September sun: his golden gleams
On gaudy flowers shine, that prank the rows
Of high-grown hollyhocks, and all tall shows
That Autumn flaunteth in his bushy bowers;
Where tomtits, hanging from the drooping heads
Of giant sunflowers, peck the nutty seeds;
And in the feathery aster bees on wing
Seize and set free the honied flowers,
Till thousand stars leap with their visiting:
While ever across the path mazily flit,
Unpiloted in the sun,
The dreamy butterflies
With dazzling colours powdered and soft glooms,
White, black and crimson stripes, and peacock eyes
Or on chance flowers sit,
With idle effort plundering one by one
The nectaries of deepest-throated blooms.

With gentle flaws the western breeze
Into the garden saileth,
Scarce here and there stirring the single trees,
For his sharpness he vaileth:
So long a comrade of the bearded corn,
Now from the stubbles whence the shocks are borne,
O'er dewy lawns he turns to stray;
As mindful of the kisses and soft play
Wherewith he enamoured the light-hearted May,

Ere he deserted her;
Lover of fragrance, and too late repents;
Nor more of heavy hyacinth now may drink,
Nor spicy pink,
Nor summer's rose, nor garnered lavender,
But the few lingering scents
Of streakèd pea, and gillyflower, and stocks
Of courtly purple, and aromatic phlox.

And at all times to hear are drowsy tones
Of dizzy flies, and humming drones,
With sudden flap of pigeon wings in the sky,
Or the wild cry
Of thirsty rooks, that scour ascare
The distant blue, to watering as they fare
With creaking pinions, or – on business bent,
If aught their ancient polity displease –
Come gathering to their colony, and there
Settling in ragged parliament,
Some stormy council hold in the high trees.

Song

by Alfred, Lord Tennyson

A spirit haunts the year's last hours
Dwelling amid these yellowing bowers.
To himself he talks;
For at eventide, listening earnestly,
At his work you may hear him sob and sigh
In the walks;
Earthward he boweth the heavy stalks
Of the mouldering flowers:
Heavily hangs the broad sunflower
Over its grave i' the earth so chilly;
Heavily hangs the hollyhock,
Heavily hangs the tiger-lily.

The air is damp, and hush'd and close
As a sick man's room when he taketh repose
An hour before death;
My very heart faints and my whole soul grieves
At the moist rich smell of the rotting leaves,
And the breath
Of the fading edges of box beneath,
And the year's last rose.
Heavily hangs the broad sunflower
Over its grave i' the earth so chilly;
Heavily hangs the hollyhock,
Heavily hangs the tiger-lily.

A DREAM OF WINTER

by W.H. Davies

These flowers survive their lover bees,
Whose deep bass voices filled the air;
The cuckoo and the nightingale
Have come and gone, we know not where.

Now, in this green and silent world,
In Autumn, full of smiling light,
I hear a bird that, suddenly,
Startles my hearing and my sight.

It is the Robin, singing of
A silver world of snow and frost;
Where all is cold and white – except
The fire that's on his own warm breast.

THISTLEDOWN

by Andrew Young

Silver against blue sky
These ghosts of day float by,
Fitful, irregular,
Each one a silk-haired star,
Till from the wind's aid freed
They settle on their seed.

Not by the famished light
Of a moon-ridden night
But by clear sunny hours
Gaily these ghosts of flowers
With rise and swirl and fall
Dance to their burial.

'CALM IS THE MORN WITHOUT A SOUND'

by Alfred, Lord Tennyson
from In Memoriam

Calm is the morn without a sound,
   Calm as to suit a calmer grief,
   And only thro' the faded leaf
The chestnut pattering to the ground;

Calm and deep peace on this high wold,
   And on these dews that drench the furze
   And all the silvery gossamers
That twinkle into green and gold:

Calm and still light on yon great plain
   That sweeps with all its autumn bowers,
   And crowded farms and lessening towers,
To mingle with the bounding main.

MORECAMBE BAY

by J.E. McMillan

Out on the islands of sand
Where only the birds' feet have marked the surface
Out on the miles of flat wetness
The gray and brown
Of windy isolation
There is a man
Digging slowly
Each spadeful of sand
Melting again to the muddy whole
The wind is very cold
On the vast plains of the bay
It skims the surface
No stronger than the white wing of a solitary gull
Pale arctic lights are in the sky
And somewhere from the other side
There might be the sucking sound of horses' hooves
Racing the tide
But silence and the sea are all
And one scrap of mankind
Like driftwood on the shore
Washed upon the estuary of the imagination.

AUTUMN: A DIRGE

by Percy Bysshe Shelley

The warm sun is failing, the bleak wind is wailing,
The bare boughs are sighing, the pale flowers are dying,
       And the Year
On the earth her death-bed, in a shroud of leaves dead,
       Is lying.
       Come, Months, come away,
       From November to May,
       In your saddest array;
       Follow the bier
       Of the dead cold Year,
And like dim shadows watch by her sepulchre.

The chill rain is falling, the nipped worm is crawling,
The rivers are swelling, the thunder is knelling
       For the Year;
The blithe swallows are flown, and the lizards each gone
       To his dwelling.
       Come, Months, come away;
       Put on white, black, and gray;
       Let your light sisters play –
       Ye, follow the bier
       Of the dead cold Year,
And make her grave green with tear on tear.

SONNET

by Herbert Read

This plain is a full arena for any eyes
Outfanning from my feet like a ribbed shell
It tinctures the interblent haze
Of autumnal moistures. A rocking bell
Peals in a gray tower filling the leafless vales
With felt sound. Falling house-reek
Scatters against the fallow fields
Or drifts into furry woods which break
The sky like black buffaloes bent
To assail the burnish-bellied clouds.
Berries in hedges are splashes split
In this massed conflict. Along the roads
Beech-boles evade the shuffling mists
Bearing into vision like sheer masts.

The Apples Ripen under Yellowing Leaves

by Thomas Caulfield Irwin

The apples ripen under yellowing leaves,
And in the farm yards by the little bay
The shadows come and go amid the sheaves,
And on the long dry inland winding way:
Where, in the thinning boughs each air bereaves,
Faint sunlights golden, and the spider weaves.
Grey are the low-laid sleepy hills, and grey
The autumn solitude of the sea day,
Where from the deep 'mid-channel, less and less
You hear along the pale east afternoon
A sound, uncertain as the silence, swoon –
The tide's sad voice ebbing toward loneliness:
And past the sands and seas' blue level line,
Ceaseless, the faint far murmur of the brine.

THE WILD SWANS AT COOLE

by W.B. Yeats

The trees are in their autumn beauty,
The woodland paths are dry,
Under the October twilight the water
Mirrors a still sky;
Upon the brimming water among the stones
Are nine-and-fifty swans.

The nineteenth autumn has come upon me
Since I first made my count;
I saw, before I had well finished,
All suddenly mount
And scatter wheeling in great broken rings
Upon their clamorous wings.

I have looked upon those brilliant creatures,
And now my heart is sore.
All's changed since I, hearing at twilight,
The first time on this shore,
The bell-beat of their wings above my head,
Trod with a lighter tread.

Unwearied still, lover by lover,
They paddle in the cold
Companionable streams or climb the air;
Their hearts have not grown old;
Passion or conquest, wander where they will,
Attend upon them still.

But now they drift on the still water,
Mysterious, beautiful;
Among what rushes will they build,
By what lake's edge or pool
Delight men's eyes when I awake some day
To find they have flown away?

Song

by Richard Watson Dixon

The feathers of the willow
Are half of them grown yellow
Above the swelling stream;
And ragged are the bushes,
And rusty are the rushes,
And wild the clouded gleam.

The thistle now is older,
His stalk begins to moulder,
His head is white as snow;
The branches all are barer,
The linnet's song is rarer,
The robin pipeth now.

FIELD OF AUTUMN

by Laurie Lee

Slow moves the acid breath of noon
over the copper-coated hill,
slow from the wild crab's bearded breast
the palsied apples fall.

Like coloured smoke the day hangs fire,
taking the village without sound;
the vulture-headed sun lies low
chained to the violet ground.

The horse upon the rocky height
rolls all the valley in his eye,
but dares not raise his foot or move
his shoulder from the fly.

The sheep, snail-backed against the wall,
lifts her blind face but does not know
the cry her blackened tongue gives forth
is the first bleat of snow.

Each bird and stone, each roof and well,
feels the gold foot of autumn pass;
each spider binds with glittering snare
the splintered bones of grass.

Slow moves the hour that sucks our life,
slow drops the late wasp from the pear,
the rose tree's thread of scent draws thin –
and snaps upon the air.

ROOKS

by Charles Sorley

There, where the rusty iron lies,
The rooks are cawing all the day.
Perhaps no man, until he dies,
Will understand them, what they say.

The evening makes the sky like clay.
The slow wind waits for night to rise.
The world is half-content. But they

Still trouble all the trees with cries,
That know, and cannot put away,
The yearning to the soul that flies
From day to night, from night to day.

PLOWMAN

by Sidney Keyes

Time was I was a plowman driving
Hard furrows, never resting, under the moon
Or in the frostbound bright-eyed morning
Labouring still; my team sleek-hided
As mulberry leaves, my team my best delight
After the sidelong blade my hero.
My iron-shod horses, my heroic walkers.
Now all that's finished. Rain's fallen now
Smudging my furrows, the comfortable
Elms are windpicked and harbour now no singer
Or southward homing bird; my horses grazing
Impossible mountain-sides, long-frogged and lonely.
And I'm gone on the roads, a peevish man
Contending with the landscape, arguing
With shrike and shrewmouse and my face in puddles;
A tiresome man not listened to nor housed
By the wise housewife, nor kissed nor handled
By any but wild weeds and summer winds.
Time was I was a fine strong fellow
Followed by girls. Now I keep company
Only with seasons and the cold crazy moon.

from **WOOD-PIGEONS**

by John Masefield

Often the woodman scares them as he comes
Swinging his axe to split the fallen birch:
The keeper with his nim-nosed dog at search
Flushes them unaware; then the hive hums.

Then from the sheddings underneath the beech,
Where squirrels rout, the flock of pigeons goes,
Their wings like sticks in battle giving blows,
The hundred hurtling to be out of reach.

Their wings flash white above a darker fan,
In drifts the colour of the smoke they pass,
They disappear above the valley grass,
They re-appear against the woodland tan.
. . . .
It is beauty none but autumn has,
These drifts of blue-grey birds whom Nature binds
Into communities of single minds,
From early leaf-fall until Candlemas.

by John Masefield

The fox knew well that, before they tore him,
They should try their speed on the downs before him.
There were three more miles to the Wan Dyke Hill,
But his heart was high that he beat them still.
The wind of the downland charmed his bones,
So off he went for the Sarsen Stones.

The pure clean air came sweet to his lungs,
Till he thought foul scorn of those crying tongues.
In a three mile more he would reach the haven
In the Wan Dyke croaked on by the raven.
In a three mile more he would make his berth
On the hard cool floor of a Wan Dyke earth,
Too deep for spade, too curved for terrier,
With the pride of the race to make rest the merrier.
In a three mile more he would reach his dream,
So his game heart gulped and he put on steam.

Like a rocket shot to a ship ashore
The lean red bolt of his body tore,
Like a ripple of wind running swift on grass;
Like a shadow on wheat when a cloud blows past,
Like a turn at the buoy in a cutter sailing
When the bright green gleam lips white at the railing.
Like the April snake whipping back to sheath,
Like the gannet's hurtle on fish beneath,
Like a kestrel chasing, like a sickle reaping,
Like all things swooping, like all things sweeping,
Like a hound for stay, like a stag for swift,
With his shadow beside like spinning drift.

On he went with a galloping rally
Past Maesbury Clump for Wan Brook Valley.
The blood in his veins went romping high,
'Get on, on, on, to the earth or die.'
The air of the downs went purely past
Till he felt the glory of going fast,
Till the terror of death, though there indeed,
Was lulled for a while by his pride of speed.
He was romping away from hounds and hunt,
He had Wan Dyke Hill and his earth in front,
In a one mile more when his point was made
He would rest in safety from dog or spade;
Nose between paws he would hear the shout
Of the 'Gone to earth!' to the hounds without,
The whine of the hounds, and their cat-feet gadding,
Scratching the earth, and their breath pad-padding:
He would hear the horn call hounds away,
And rest in peace till another day.

Autumn

Anonymous (1753)

I at my window sit, and see
Autumn his russet fingers lay
  On ev'ry leaf of ev'ry tree.
I call, but Summer will not stay.

  She flies, the boasting goddess flies,
And, pointing where th'espaliers shoot,
    'Deserve my parting gift' she cries,
'I take the leaves but not the fruit.'

  Let me the parting gift improve,
And emulate the just reply,
  As life's short seasons swift remove,
Ere fixed in Winter's frost I lie.

  Health, beauty, vigour now decline,
The pride of Summer's splendid day,
  Leaves, which the stem must now resign,
The mournful prelude of decay.

  But let fair Virtue's fruit remain,
Though Summer with my leaves be fled;
  Then, not despised, I'll not complain,
But cherish Autumn in her stead.

THE SHEAF

by Andrew Young

I'd often seen before
That sheaf of corn hung from the bough –
Strange in a wood a sheaf of corn
Though by the winds half torn
And thrashed by rain to empty straw.
And then today I saw
A small pink twitching snout
And eyes like black beads sewn in fur
Peep from a hole in doubt,
And heard on dry leaves go tat-tat
The stiff tail of the other rat.
And now as the short day grows dim
And here and there farms in the dark
Turn to a spark,
I on my stumbling way think how
With indistinguishable limb
And tight tail round each other's head
They'll make tonight one ball in bed,
Those long-tailed lovers who have come
To share the pheasants' harvest-home.

Pheasant

by Sidney Keyes

Cock stubble-searching pheasant, delicate
Stepper, Cathayan bird, you fire
The landscape, as across the hollow lyre
Quick fingers burn the moment: call your mate
From the deep woods tonight, for your surprised
Metallic summons answers me like wire
Thrilling with messages, and I cannot wait
To catch its evening import, half-surmised.
Others may speak these things, but you alone
Fear never noise, make the damp thickets ring
With your assertions, set the afternoon
Alight with coloured pride. Your image glows
At autumn's centre – bright, unquestioning
Exotic bird, haunter of autumn hedgerows.

OCTOBER TREES

by Siegfried Sassoon

How innocent were these
Trees, that in mist-green May,
Blown by a prospering breeze,
Stood garlanded and gay;
Who now in sundown glow
Of serious colour clad
Confront me with their show
As though resigned and sad.

Trees who unwhispering stand
Umber and bronze and gold,
Pavilioning the land
For one grown tired and old;
Elm, chestnut, beech and lime,
I am merged in you, who tell
Once more in tones of time
Your foliaged farewell.

LAPWING

by Rex Warner

Leaves, summer's coinage spent, golden are all together
  whirled,
sent spinning, dipping, slipping, shuffled by heavy handed
  wind,
shifted sideways, sifted, lifted, and in swarms made to fly,
spent sunflies, gorgeous tatters, airdrift, pinions of trees.

Pennons of the autumn wind, flying the same loose flag,
minions of the rush of air, companions of draggled cloud,
tattered, scattered pell mell, diving, with side-slip suddenly
  wailing
as they scale the uneasy sky flapping the lapwing fly.

Plover, with under the tail pine-red, deaf leafwealth in down
  displayed,
crested with glancing crests, sheeny with seagreen, mirror of
  movement
of the deep sea horses plunging, restless, fretted by the whip of
  wind,
tugging green tons, we waste, lugging a mass to Labrador.

See them fall wailing over high hill tops with hue and cry,
like uneasy ghosts slipping in the dishevelled air,
with ever so much of forlorn ocean and wastes of wind
in their elbowing of the air and their lamentable call.

ONE DAY OF AUTUMN

by Charles Tomlinson

One day of autumn
sun had uncongealed
the frost that clung
wherever shadows spread
their arctic greys among
October grass: mid-
field an oak still
held its foliage intact
but then began
releasing leaf by leaf
full half,
till like a startled
flock they scattered
on the wind: and one
more venturesome than all
the others shone far out
a moment in mid-air,
before it glittered off
and sheered into the dip
a stream ran through
to disappear with it

Song

by Emily Brontë

Fall, leaves, fall; die, flowers, away;
Lengthen night and shorten day;
Every leaf speaks bliss to me
Fluttering from the autumn tree.
I shall smile when wreaths of snow
Blossom where the rose should grow;
I shall sing when night's decay
Ushers in a drearier day.

Last Week in October

by Thomas Hardy

The trees are undressing, and fling in many places –
On the gray road, the roof, the window-sill –
Their radiant robes and ribbons and yellow laces;
A leaf each second so is flung at will,
Here, there, another and another, still and still.

A spider's web has caught one while downcoming,
That stays there dangling when the rest pass on;
Like a suspended criminal hangs he, mumming
In golden garb, while one yet green, high yon,
Trembles, as fearing such a fate for himself anon.

LEAF

by Gwyn Thomas

The leaf from the tree is shed.
It hovers, it flies,
Holds onto the breeze,
Gently hangs,
Quietly swims,
Slides – a bright flash –
White-bellied or yellow
It clowns, whirling with colours,
Fantastic it flaunts
To mouse shortfooted, gurgling tints,
It wheels, it slants,
Bright it swings downward.
The leaf from the tree is shed –
And what's it do?
        It dies.

Translated from the Welsh by
Tony Conran

'DOWN FROM THE BRANCHES FALL THE LEAVES'

Anonymous (c. 13th century)

Down from the branches fall the leaves,
A wanness comes on all the trees,
The summer's done;
And into his last house in heaven
Now goes the sun.

Sharp frost destroys the tender sprays,
Birds are a-cold in these short days.
The nightingale
Is grieving that the fire of heaven
Is now grown pale.

The swollen river rushes on
Past meadows whence the green has gone,
The golden sun
Has fled our world. Snow falls by day,
The nights are numb.

AUTUMN SONG

by Laurence Binyon

All is wild with change,
Large the yellow leaves
Hang, so frail and few.
Now they go, they too
Flutter, lifted, lying,
Everywhither strewn.
All is wild with change.

Nothing shrinks or grieves.
There's no time for sighing.
Night comes fast on noon,
Dawn treads after soon;
Days are springing, dying,
We with them are flying.
All is wild with change.

THE ELM-BEETLE

by Andrew Young

So long I sat and conned
That naked bole
With the strange hieroglyphics scored
That those small priests,
The beetle-grubs, had bored,
Telling of gods and kings and beasts
And the long journey of the soul
Through magic-opened gates
To where the throned Osiris waits,
That when at last I woke
I stepped from an Egyptian tomb
To see the wood's sun-spotted gloom,
And rising cottage smoke
That leaned upon the wind and broke,
Roller-striped fields, and smooth cow-shadowed pond.

THE BURNING OF THE LEAVES

by Laurence Binyon

Now is the time for the burning of the leaves.
They go to the fire; the nostril pricks with smoke
Wandering slowly into a weeping mist.
Brittle and blotched, ragged and rotten sheaves!
A flame seizes the smouldering ruin and bites
On stubborn stalks that crackle as they resist.

The last hollyhock's fallen tower is dust;
All the spices of June are a bitter reek,
All the extravagant riches spent and mean.
All burns! The reddest rose is a ghost;
Sparks whirl up, to expire in the mist: the wild
Fingers of fire are making corruption clean.

Now is the time for stripping the spirit bare,
Time for the burning of days ended and done,
Idle solace of things that have gone before:
Rootless hopes and fruitless desire are there;
Let them go to the fire, with never a look behind.
The world that was ours is a world that is ours no more.

They will come again, the leaf and the flower, to arise
From squalor of rottenness into the old splendour,
And magical scents to a wondering memory bring;
The same glory, to shine upon different eyes.
Earth cares for her own ruins, naught for ours.
Nothing is certain, only the certain spring.

HUNTING THE HARE

Welsh folk song

It's the hare that we go hunting
On a fine and bracing day.
From the furze she's just been started –
Dogs and puss are both away.
Like the wind, or maybe faster,
After hare and hounds we go,
Dodging through the upland sheeptracks
Such a clever to and fro.

Running for her life by hedges
Skirts the edges of the groves;
Greyhound looks as if he's flying,
Hare is just beyond his nose!
Long may hunting be our pastime,
Wine and feasting, songs and tales –
Stories of the ninefold huntings
Ringing round the land of Wales.

Translated by Tony Conran

PARTRIDGES

by John Masefield

Here they lie mottled to the ground unseen,
This covey linked together from the nest.
The nosing pointers put them from their rest,
The wings whirr, the guns flash and all has been.

The lucky crumple to the clod, shot clean,
The wounded drop and hurry and lie close;
The sportsmen praise the pointer and his nose,
Until he scents the hiders and is keen.

Tumbled in bag with rabbits, pigeons, hares,
The crumpled corpses have forgotten all
The covey's joys of strong or gliding flight.

But when the planet lamps the coming night,
The few survivors seek those friends of theirs;
The twilight hears and darkness hears them call.

'WHEN THE WATER FOWL ARE FOUND, THE FALCONERS HASTEN'

Anonymous (14th century)
from *The Parliament of the Three Ages* (ll. 210–45)

When the water fowl are found, the falconers hasten
To untie the leashes and let the hawks loose.
They snatch off their hoods and cast them from their hand,
And the hottest in haste quickly soar up high,
With their bells so bright ringing blithe and bold,
And there they hover aloft like angels in heaven.
Then the falconers furiously rush to the river
Where at the water they rouse up the fowl with their rods,
Raining blows all round them to service their hawks.
Then the tercelets swiftly strike down the teals,
And the tanners and lannerets swoop to the ducks,
Meeting the mallards and striking down many.
The hawks in the air hurtle down from on high,
And they hit the heron, whooped up by the falconers,
Buffet him, beat him, and bring him to the ground,
And assail him savagely and boldly seize him.
Then the falconers set out in hasty pursuit,
And run up hurriedly to give help to their hawks,
For with the bit of his bill the heron slashes about.
They drop down to their knees and crawl in cautiously,
Catch hold of his wings and wrench them together,
Burst open the bones and break them apart.
He picks out the marrow onto his glove with a quill,
And whoops them to the quarry that they crushed to death.

He feeds them and quiets them, and then loudly calls out,
Encouraging those on the wing to give up the hunt,
Then takes them on his hand and slips on their hoods,
Tightens up the thongs that secure their caps,
And loops in their leashes through rings of silver.
Then he picks up his lure and looks to his horse,
And leaps up on the left side as called for by custom.
The carriers quickly put up the game fowl,
And wait for the tercelets that often are troublesome,
For some choose the chase, though others are better.
The mud-splashed spaniels keep springing about,
Bedraggled from their dunking when the ducks took to the water.

Translated by Peggy Munsterberg

'MILES, AND MILES, AND MILES OF DESOLATION'

by Algernon Charles Swinburne
from By the North Sea

Miles, and miles, and miles of desolation!
   Leagues on leagues on leagues without a change!
Sign or token of some eldest nation
   Here would make the strange land not so strange.
Time-forgotten, yea since time's creation,
   Seem these borders where the sea-birds range.

Slowly, gladly, full of peace and wonder
   Grows his heart who journeys here alone.
Earth and all its thoughts of earth sink under
   Deep as deep in water sinks a stone.
Hardly knows it if the rollers thunder,
   Hardly whence the lonely wind is blown.

Tall the plumage of the rush-flower tosses,
   Sharp and soft in many a curve and line
Gleam and glow the sea-coloured marsh-mosses
   Salt and splendid from the circling brine.
Streak on streak of glimmering seashine crosses
   All the land sea-saturate as with wine.

175

SALISBURY PLAIN

by Edward Lucie-Smith

Their heads bent down before the polar wind
From ridge to ridge two labourers cross the plough,
Smoke from a bonfire creeps along the ground,
Saplings and hedgerows tangled in its flow.

And fifty miles away the Channel gale
Beats in the bays; with loud metallic cries,
Wings spread and rigid, seagulls turn and sail
Sideways to leeward, fly as paper flies.

With furrows for the waves of a brown sea
The land heaves up, and tries to change its form;
Leaves fallen rise like spindrift, and the storm
Roars about forts and barrows which have stood
Three thousand years; it batters in the wood
As if to overthrow the Druids' tree.

'BUGLES BLEW THE TRIUMPH, HORNS BLARED LOUD'

Anonymous (?14th century)
from *Sir Gawain and the Green Knight*

Bugles blew the triumph, horns blared loud.
There was hallooing in high pride by all present;
Braches bayed at the beast, as bidden by their masters,
The chief huntsman in charge of that chase so hard.
Then one who was wise in wood-crafts
Started in style to slash open the boar.
First he hewed off the head and hoisted it on high,
Then rent him roughly along the ridge of his back,
Brought out the bowels and broiled them on coals
For blending with bread as the braches' reward.
Then he broke out the brawn from the bright broad flanks,
Took out the offal, as is fit,
Attached the two halves entirely together,
And on a strong stake stoutly hung them.
Then home they hurried with huge beast,
With the boar's head borne before the baron himself,
Who had destroyed him in the stream by the strength of his arm.

Translated by Brian Stone

AUTUMN IDLENESS

by Dante Gabriel Rossetti

This sunlight shames November where he grieves
   In dead red leaves, and will not let him shun
   The day, though bough with bough be over-run.
But with a blessing every glade receives
High salutation; while from hillock-eaves
   The deer gaze calling, dappled white and dun,
   As if, being foresters of old, the sun
Had marked them with the shade of forest-leaves.

Here dawn to-day unveiled her magic glass;
   Here noon now gives the thirst and takes the dew;
Till eve bring rest when other good things pass.
   And here the lost hours the lost hours renew
While I still lead my shadow o'er the grass,
   Nor know, for longing, that which I should do.

DEER

by John Drinkwater

Shy in their herding dwell the fallow deer.
They are spirits of wild sense. Nobody near
Comes upon their pastures. There a life they live,
Of sufficient beauty, phantom, fugitive,
Treading as in jungles free leopards do,
Printless as evelight, instant as dew.
The great kine are patient, and home-coming sheep
Know our bidding. The fallow deer keep
Delicate and far their counsels wild,
Never to be folded reconciled
To the spoiling hand as the poor flocks are;
Lightfoot, and swift, and unfamiliar,
These you may not hinder, unconfined
Beautiful flocks of the mind.

WATERFALL

by Seamus Heaney

The burn drowns steadily in its own downpour,
A helter-skelter of muslin and glass
That skids to a halt, crashing up suds.

Simultaneous acceleration
And sudden braking; water goes over
Like villains dropped screaming to justice.

It appears an athletic glacier
Has reared into reverse: is swallowed up
And regurgitated through this long throat.

My eye rides over and downwards, falls with
Hurtling tons that slabber and spill,
Falls, yet records the tumult thus standing still.

INVERSNAID

by Gerard Manley Hopkins

This darksome burn, horseback brown,
His rollrock highroad roaring down,
In coop and in comb the fleece of his foam
Flutes and low to the lake falls home.

A windpuff-bonnet of fawn-froth
Turns and twindles over the broth
Of a pool so pitchblack, fell frowning,
It rounds and rounds Despair to drowning.

Degged with dew, dappled with dew
Are the groins of the braes that the brook treads through
Wiry heathpacks, flitches of fern,
And the beadbonny ash that sits over the burn.

What would the world be, once bereft
Of wet and of wildness? Let them be left,
O let them be left, wildness and wet;
Long live the weeds and the wilderness yet.

HIGH ABOVE THE HIGHLAND GLEN

by Will H. Ogilvie

High above the Highland glen
Flamed and burned the purple heather
Colours never mixed of men
Tints no painter put together.

And I guessed that, where I trod,
Quaffing his Olympian gill
Rudely had some reeling God
Spilt his wine-cup on the hill.

THE FORK OF THE ROAD

by William Renton

An utter moorland, high, and wide, and flat;
A beaten roadway, branching out in grave distaste;
And weather-beaten and defaced,
Pricking its ears along the solitary waste –
A signpost; pointing this way, pointing that.

SOWING

by Edward Thomas

It was a perfect day
For sowing; just
As sweet and dry was the ground
As tobacco-dust.

I tasted deep the hour
Between the far
Owl's chuckling first soft cry
And the first star.

A long stretched hour it was;
Nothing undone
Remained; the early seeds
All safely sown.

And now, hark at the rain,
Windless and light,
Half a kiss, half a tear,
Saying good-night.

THE WAY OF THE WIND

by Algernon Charles Swinburne

The wind's way in the deep sky's hollow
None may measure, as none can say
How the heart in her shows the swallow
  The wind's way.

Hope nor fear can avail to stay
Waves that whiten on wrecks that wallow,
Times and seasons that wane and slay.

Life and love, till the strong night swallow
Thought and hope and the red last ray,
Swim the waters of years that follow
  The wind's way.

Octboer

by Charles Tomlinson

Autumn seems ending: there is lassitude
Wherever ripeness has not filled its brood
Of rinds and rounds: all promises are fleshed
Or now they fail. Far gone, these blackberries –
For each one that you pull, two others fall
Full of themselves, the leaves slick with their ooze:
Awaiting cold, we welcome in the frost
To cleanse these purples, this discandying,
As eagerly as we shall look to spring.

AUTUMN EVENING

by John Clare

I love to hear the autumn crows go by
And see the starnels darken down the sky;
The bleaching stack the bustling sparrow leaves,
And plops with merry note beneath the eaves.
The odd and lated pigeon bounces by,
As if a wary watching hawk was nigh,
While far and fearing nothing, high and slow,
The stranger birds to distant places go;
While short of flight the evening robin comes
To watch the maiden sweeping out the crumbs,
Nor fears the idle shout of passing boy,
But pecks about the door, and sings for joy;
Then in the hovel where the cows are fed
Finds till the morning comes a pleasant bed.

Autumn

by Thomas Ernest Hulme

A touch of cold in the Autumn night –
I walked abroad,
And saw the ruddy moon lean over a hedge
Like a red-faced farmer.
I did not stop to speak, but nodded,
And round about were the wistful stars
With white faces like town children.

MOONLIT APPLES

by John Drinkwater

At the top of the house the apples are laid in rows,
And the skylight lets the moonlight in, and those
Apples are deep-sea apples of green. There goes
A cloud on the moon in the autumn night.

A mouse in the wainscot scratches, and scratches, and then
There is no sound at the top of the house of men
Or mice; and the cloud is blown, and the moon again
Dapples the apples with deep-sea light.

They are lying in rows there, under the gloomy beams;
On the sagging floor; they gather the silver streams
Out of the moon, those moonlit apples of dreams,
And quiet is the steep stair under.

In the corridors under there is nothing but sleep.
And stiller than ever on orchard boughs they keep
Tryst with the moon, and deep is the silence, deep
On moon-washed apples of wonder.

THE WHITE OWL

by F.J. Patmore

When night is o'er the wood
  And moon-scared watch-dogs howl,
Comes forth in search of food
  The snowy mystic owl.
His soft, white, ghostly wings
  Beat noiselessly the air
Like some lost soul that hopelessly
  Is mute in its despair.

But now his hollow note
  Rings cheerless through the glade
And o'er the silent moat
  He flits from shade to shade.
He hovers, swoops and glides
  O'er meadows, moors and streams;
He seems to be some fantasy –
  A ghostly bird of dreams.

Why dost thou haunt the night?
  Why dost thou love the moon
When other birds delight
  To sing their joy at noon?
Art thou then crazed with love,
  Or is't for some fell crime
That thus thou flittest covertly
  At this unhallowed time?

WILD DUCK

by Euros Bowen

Ducks are like seed the dawn-sower scatters
   To the garden of still water;
Nightfall on gravel provokes them,
They rise, they flower from the lake.

Translated from the Welsh by
Tony Conran

T o   N i g h t

by Thomas Lovell Beddoes

So thou art come again, old black-winged Night,
Like an huge bird, between us and the sun,
Hiding, with out-stretched form, the genial light;
And still, beneath thine icy bosom's dun
And cloudy plumage, hatching fog-breathed blight,
And embryo storms, and crabbed frosts, that shun
Day's warm caress. The owls from ivied loop
Are shrieking homage, as thou cowerest high,
Like sable cow pausing in eager stoop
On the dim world thou gluttest thy clouded eye,
Silently waiting latest time's fell whoop
When thou shalt quit thine eyrie in the sky,
To pounce upon the world with eager claw,
And tomb time, death, and substance in thy maw.

THE WANING MOON

by Percy Bysshe Shelley

And like a dying lady, lean and pale,
Who totters forth, wrapt in a gauzy veil,
Out of her chamber, led by the insane
And feeble wanderings of her fading brain,
The moon arose up in the murky East,
A white and shapeless mass —

MY STORY

Anonymous (7th century)

Here's my story; the stag cries,
Winter snarls as summer dies.

The wind bullies the low sun
In poor light; the seas moan.

Shapeless bracken is turning red,
The wildgoose raises its desperate head.

Bird's wings freeze where fields are hoary.
The world is ice. That's my story.

Translated from the Irish by
Brendan Kennelly

WINTER

He has hanged himself – the Sun.
He dangles
A scarecrow in thin air.

He is dead for love – the Sun;
He who in forest tangles
Wooed all things fair

That great lover – the Sun,
Now spangles
The wood with blood-stains.

He has hanged himself – the Sun.
How thin he dangles
In these gray rains!

November
F.W. Harvey

'AND NOW, IF THE NIGHT SHALL BE COLD, ACROSS THE SKY'

by Robert Bridges
from *November*

And now, if the night shall be cold, across the sky
Linnets and twites, in small flocks helter-skelter,
All the afternoon to the gardens fly,
From thistle-pastures hurrying to gain the shelter
Of American rhododendron or cherry-laurel:
And here and there, near chilly setting of sun,
In an isolated tree a congregation
Of starlings chatter and chide,
Thickset as summer leaves, in garrulous quarrel:
Suddenly they hush as one –
The tree top springs –
And off, with a whirr of wings,
They fly by the score
To the holly-thicket, and there with myriads more
Dispute for the roosts; and from the unseen nation
A babel of tongues, like running water unceasing,
Makes live the wood, the flocking cries increasing,
Wrangling discordantly, incessantly,
While falls the night on them self-occupied;
The long dark night, that lengthens slow,
Deepening with winter to starve grass and tree,
And soon to bury in snow
The Earth, that, sleeping 'neath her frozen stole,
Shall dream a dream crept from the sunless pole
Of how her end shall be.

'HEAR NEXT OF WINTER'

by *Vita Sackville-West*
from *The Land*

Hear next of winter, when the florid summer,
The bright barbarian scarfed in a swathe of flowers,
The corn a golden ear-ring on her cheek,
Has left our north to winter's finer etching,
To raw-boned winter, when the sun
Slinks in a narrow and a furtive arc,
Red as the harvest moon, from east to west,
And the swans go home at dusk to the leaden lake
Dark in the plains of snow.

Water alone remains untouched by snow.

Here is no colour, here but form and structure,
The bones of trees, the magpie bark of birches,
Apse of trees and tracery of network,
Fields of snow and tranquil trees in snow
Through veils of twilight, northern, still, and sad,
Waiting for night, and for the moon
Riding the sky and turning snow to beauty,
Pale in herself as winter's very genius,
Casting the shadows delicate of trees,
Moon-shadows on the moon-lit snow, the ghost
Of shadows, veering with the moving moon,
Faint as the markings on the silver coin
Risen in heaven, – shades of barren ranges,
Craters, and lunar Apennines, and plains
Old as the earth, and cold as space, and empty,
Whence Earth appears a planet far surpassing

198

Our ken of any star for neighbouring splendour,
Her continents, her seas, her mountain ranges
Splendid and visible, majestic planet
Sweeping through space, and bearing in her train
Her silver satellite that sees no strife,
No warring of her men, no grief, no anger,
No blood spilt red to stain the golden planet,
But sees her architecture royally:
Dark Asia; islands; spread of the Pacific,
The silver satellite that casts the ghost
Of ghostly trees across the fields of snow.

Now in the radiant night no men are stirring:
The little houses sleep with shuttered panes;
Only the hares are wakeful, loosely loping
Along the hedges with their easy gait,
And big loose ears, and pad-prints crossing snow;
The ricks and trees stand silent in the moon,
Loaded with snow, and tiny drifts from branches
Slip to the ground in woods with sliding sigh.
Private the woods, enjoying a secret beauty.

THE CRISP FROST LIES WHITE AND HOARY

by Anthony Bowen Fletcher

The crisp frost lies white and hoary
Naked trees swathed in mist
Suddenly by sunshine kissed
Awake in all their Autumn glory.

The squirrel takes a last look round
Birds search the fresh turned furrow
Badger and fieldmouse deeper burrow
And robin presents his song new found.

The sun is like a ball of fire
Air is chill and breath does show
As homeward from the fields horses go
The silver moon rises ever higher.

OLD MARTINMAS EVE

by Ivor Gurney

The moon, one tree, one star.
Still meadows far,
Enwreathed and scarfed by phantom lines of white.
November's night
Of all her nights, I thought, and turned to see
Again that moon and star-supporting tree.
If some most quiet tune had spoken then;
Some silver thread of sounds; a core within
That sea-deep silentness, I had not known
Even such joy in peace, but sound was none —
Nor should be till birds roused to find the dawn.

'DAY'

by Robert Browning
from Pippa Passes

Day!
Faster and more fast,
O'er night's brim, day boils at last:
Boils, pure gold, o'er the cloud-cup's brim
Where spurting and suppressed it lay,
For not a froth-flake touched the rim
Of yonder gap in the solid gray
Of the eastern cloud, an hour away;
But forth one wavelet, then another, curled,
Till the whole sunrise, not to be suppressed,
Rose, reddened, and its seething breast
Flickered in bounds, grew gold, then overflowed the world.

from **WINTER SUNDAY**

by David Holbrook

So severe this black frost that it bent
The white burred burden of asparagus,
Hooped the old docks and broke the thistle's spent
Grey screws of spike and floss.

They lay rimed in their torment in each bed:
And as an epilogue
I heard a voice speak, and I turned my head
Only to see a leaf fall in the fog

Down the drained sycamore, like a withered hand,
Bough by bough, to the earth. No sound
But these few vacant yellow cackles, and
A dripping where the frost's grip was unwound.

THE LAST OF NIGHT

by Charles Tomlinson

Mist after frost. The woodlands
stretch vague in it, but catch
the rising light on reefs
of foliage above the greyish
'sea' I was about to say,
but sun so rapidly advances
between glance and word,
under that leafy headland
mist lies a sea no more:
a gauze visibly fading
burns out to nothing, lets grow
beneath each mid-field bush
a perfect shadow, and among
frost-whitened tussocks
the last of night recedes along
tracks the animals have taken
back into earth and wood.

'SOON AS THE SILENT SHADES OF NIGHT WITHDREW'

by Ambrose Philips
from *A Winter-Piece*

Soon as the silent shades of night withdrew,
The ruddy morn disclosed at once to view
The face of nature in a rich disguise,
And brightened ev'ry object to my eyes.
For ev'ry shrub, and ev'ry blade of grass,
And ev'ry pointed thorn, seemed wrought in glass;
In pearls and rubies rich the hawthorns show,
While through the ice the crimson berries glow.
The thick-sprung reeds the wat'ry marshes yield
Seem polished lances in a hostile field.
The stag in limpid currents, with surprise,
Sees crystal branches on his forehead rise.
The spreading oak, the beech and tow'ring pine,
Glazed over, in the freezing ether shine:
The frighted birds the rattling branches shun,
That wave and glitter in the distant sun.
    When, if a sudden gust of wind arise,
The brittle forest into atoms flies;
The crackling wood beneath the tempest bends,
And in a spangled show'r the prospect ends;
Or, if a southern gale the region warm,
And by degrees unbind the wintry charm,
The traveller a miry country sees,
And journeys sad beneath the dropping trees.

A HARD FROST

by C. Day Lewis

A frost came in the night and stole my world
And left this changeling for it – a precocious
Image of spring, too brilliant to be true:
White lilac on the windowpane, each grass-blade
Furred like a catkin, maydrift loading the hedge.
The elms behind the house are elms no longer
But blossomers in crystal, stems of the mist
That hangs yet in the valley below, amorphous
As the blind tissue whence creation formed.

   The sun looks out, and the fields blaze with diamonds.
Mockery spring, to lend this bridal gear
For a few hours to a raw country maid,
Then leave her all disconsolate with old fairings
Of aconite and snowdrop! No, not here
Amid this flounce and filigree of death
Is the real transformation scene in progress,
But deep below where frost
Worrying the stiff clods unclenches their
Grip on the seed and lets our future breathe.

NOVEMBER

by Hartley Coleridge

The mellow year is hasting to its close;
The little birds have almost sung their last,
Their small notes twitter in the dreary blast —
That shrill-piped harbinger of early snows;
The patient beauty of the scentless rose,
Oft with the morn's hoar crystal quaintly glassed,
Hangs, a pale mourner for the summer past,
And makes a little summer where it grows:
In the chill sunbeam of the faint brief day
The dusky waters shudder as they shine,
The russet leaves obstruct the straggling way
Of oozy brooks, which no deep banks define,
And the gaunt woods, in ragged, scant array,
Wrap their old limbs with sombre ivy twine.

THE BULLFINCH

by Betty Hughes

I saw upon a winter's day
A bullfinch on a hedgerow spray;
He piped one note.
And since the countryside was mute,
As pure as rain I heard the flute
Of that small throat.

He picked a rotting willow-seed;
He whistled, in his joy to feed,
A whole sweet stave.
His sloe-black head, how shining sleek,
How strong his blunted sooty beak,
His eyes, how brave.

Then boldly down he came to drink
Out of a roadside puddle's brink,
Half ice, half mud;
So coral-breasted, sturdy, merry,
That I forgave him plum and cherry
Nipped in the bud.

THE GALLOWS

by Edward Thomas

There was a weasel lived in the sun
With all his family,
Till a keeper shot him with his gun
And hung him up on a tree,
Where he swings in the wind and rain,
In the sun and in the snow,
Without pleasure, without pain,
On the dead oak tree bough.

There was a crow who was no sleeper,
But a thief and a murderer
Till a very late hour; and this keeper
Made him one of the things that were,
To hang and flap in rain and wind,
In the sun and in the snow,
There are no more sins to be sinned
On the dead oak tree bough.

There was a magpie, too,
Had a long tongue and a long tail;
He could both talk and do –
But what did that avail?
He, too, flaps in the wind and rain
Alongside weasel and crow,
Without pleasure, without pain,
On the dead oak tree bough.

And many other beasts
And birds, skin, bone and feather,
Have been taken from their feasts
But hung up there together,
To swing and have endless leisure
In the sun and in the snow,
Without pain, without pleasure,
On the dead oak tree bough.

Sonnet XXV

by Hilaire Belloc

It freezes: all across a soundless sky
The birds go home. The governing dark's begun.
The steadfast dark that waits not for a sun;
The ultimate dark wherein the race shall die.
Death with his evil finger to his lip
Leers in at human windows, turning spy
To learn the country where his rule shall lie
When he assumes perpetual generalship.

The undefeated enemy, the chill
That shall benumb the voiceful earth at last,
Is master of our moment, and has bound
The viewless wind itself. There is no sound.
It freezes. Every friendly stream is fast.
It freezes, and the graven twigs are still.

from **THE WINTERS SPRING**

by John Clare

I never want the christmas rose
To come before its time
The seasons each as God bestows
Are simple and sublime
I love to see the snow storm hing
'Tis but the winter garb of Spring

I never want the grass to bloom
The snow-storm's best in white
I love to see the tempest come
And love its piercing light
The dazzled eyes that love to cling
O'er snow white meadows sees the Spring

I love the snow the crimpling snow
That hangs on every thing
It covers every thing below
Like white doves brooding wing
A landscape to the aching sight
A vast expance of dazzling light

It is the foliage of the woods
That winter's bring – The dress
White easter of the year in bud
That makes the winter Spring
The frost and snow his poseys bring
Natures white spirits of the Spring.

GIFTS OF SILENCE

by Laurence Binyon

No sound in all the mountains, all the sky!
Yet hush! one delicate sound, minutely clear,
Makes the immense Silence draw more near, —
Some secret ripple of running water, shy
As a delight that hides from alien eye:
And the encircling mountains seem an ear
Only for this; the still clouds hang to hear
All music in a sound small as a sigh.

For below rises to the horizon rim
The silent sea. Above, those gray clouds pile;
But through them tremblingly escape, like bloom,
Like buds of beams, for sleepy mile on mile,
Wellings of light, as if heaven had not room
For the hidden glory and must overbrim.

THE MAIN-DEEP

by James Stephens

The long-rólling,
Steady-póuring,
Deep-trenchéd
Green billów:

The wide-topped,
Unbróken,
Green-glacid,
Slow-sliding,

Cold-flushing,
– On – on – on –
Chill-rushing,
Hush–hushing,

. . . Hush–hushing . . .

PERFECT
ON THE WESTERN SEABOARD
OF SOUTH UIST

by Hugh MacDiarmid

Los muertos abren los ojos a los que viven

I found a pigeon's skull on the machair,
All the bones pure white and dry, and chalky,
But perfect,
Without a crack or a flaw anywhere.

At the back, rising out of the beak,
Were domes like bubbles of thin bone,
Almost transparent, where the brain had been
That fixed the tilt of the wings.

With the exception of the first line, the words of 'Perfect' were taken from 'Porth-y-Rhyd', a short story in a collection by Glyn Jones entitled *The Blue Bed*, published by Jonathan Cape in 1937.

WINTER SEASCAPE

by John Betjeman

The sea runs back against itself
With scarcely time for breaking wave
To cannonade a slatey shelf
And thunder under in a cave

Before the next can fully burst.
The headwind, blowing harder still,
Smooths it to what it was at first —
A slowly rolling water-hill.

Against the breeze the breakers haste,
Against the tide their ridges run
And all the sea's a dappled waste
Criss-crossing underneath the sun.

Far down the beach the ripples drag
Blown backward, rearing from the shore,
And wailing gull and shrieking shag
Alone can pierce the ocean roar.

Unheard, a mongrel hound gives tongue,
Unheard are shouts of little boys:
What chance has any inland lung
Against this multi-water noise?

Here where the cliffs alone prevail
I stand exultant, neutral, free,
And from the cushion of the gale
Behold a huge consoling sea.

HIGH WAVING HEATHER

by Emily Brontë

High waving heather 'neath stormy blasts bending,
Midnight and moonlight and bright shining stars,
Darkness and glory rejoicingly blending,
Earth rising to heaven and heaven descending,
Man's spirit away from its drear dungeon sending,
Bursting the fetters and breaking the bars.

All down the mountain sides wild forests lending
One mighty voice to the life-giving wind,
Rivers their banks in the jubilee rending,
Fast through the valleys a reckless course wending,
Wider and deeper their waves extending,
Leaving a desolate desert behind.

Shining and lowering and swelling and dying,
Changing forever from midnight to noon;
Roaring like thunder, like soft music sighing,
Shadows on shadows advancing and flying,
Lightning-bright flashes the deep gloom defying,
Coming as swiftly and fading as soon.

A FROSTY DAY

by John Leicester Warren, Lord de Tabley

Grass afield wears silver thatch;
   Palings all are edged with rime;
Frost-flowers pattern round the latch;
   Cloud nor breeze dissolve the clime;

When the waves are solid floor,
   And the clods are iron-bound,
And the boughs are crystall'd hoar,
   And the red leaf nailed a-ground.

When the fieldfare's flight is slow,
   And a rosy vapour rim,
Now the sun is small and low,
   Belts along the region dim.

When the ice-crack flies and flaws,
   Shore to shore, with thunder shock,
Deeper than the evening daws,
   Clearer than the village clock.

When the rusty blackbird strips,
   Bunch by bunch, the coral thorn;
And the pale day-crescent dips,
   New to heaven, a slender horn.

THE WINTER FLOWER

by John Henry Newman

Bloom, beloved Flower! –
  Unknown; – 'tis no matter.
Courts glitter brief hour,
  Crowds can but flatter.

Plants in the garden
  See best the Sun's glory;
They miss the green sward in
  A conservatory.

– PRIZED WHERE'ER KNOWN. –
  Sure this is a blessing,
Outrings the loud tone
  Of the dull world's caressing.

'THE STREAMS ARE LOST AMID THE SPLENDID BLANK'

by *William Cowper*
from *The Task* (Book V: The Winter Morning Walk)

The streams are lost amid the splendid blank,
O'erwhelming all distinction. On the flood,
Indurated and fixed, the snowy weight
Lies undissolved; while silently beneath,
And unperceived, the current steals away.
Not so where, scornful of a check, it leaps
The mill-dam, dashes on the restless wheel,
And wantons in the pebbly gulf below:
No frost can bind it there; its utmost force
Can but arrest the light and smoky mist
That in its fall the liquid sheet throws wide.
And see where it has hung th'embroidered banks
With forms so various, that no pow'rs of art,
The pencil or the pen, may trace the scene!
Here glitt'ring turrets rise, upbearing high
(Fantastic misarrangement!) on the roof
Large growth of what may seem the sparkling trees
And shrubs of fairy land. The crystal drops
That trickle down the branches, fast congealed,
Shoot onto pillars of pellucid length,
And prop the pile they but adorned before.
Here grotto within grotto safe defies
The sun-beam; there, embossed and fretted wild,
The growing wonder takes a thousand shapes
Capricious, in which fancy seeks in vain
The likeness of some object seen before.
Thus nature works as if to mock at art,
And in defiance of her rival pow'rs . . .

'A WIDOW BIRD SATE MOURNING FOR HER LOVE'

by Percy Bysshe Shelley
from Charles the First

'A widow bird sate mourning for her love
    Upon a wintry bough;
The frozen wind crept on above,
    The freezing stream below.

There was no leaf upon the forest bare,
    No flower upon the ground,
And little motion in the air
    Except the mill-wheel's sound.'

IF THOU WAST STILL

by *Richard Watson Dixon*

If thou wast still, O stream,
    Thou would'st be frozen now:
And 'neath an icy shield
    Thy current warm would flow.

But wild thou art and rough;
    And so the bitter breeze,
That chafes thy shuddering waves,
    May never bid thee freeze.

A WINDY DAY

by Andrew Young

This wind brings all dead things to life,
Branches that lash the air like whips
And dead leaves rolling in a hurry
Or peering in a rabbits' bury
Or trying to push down a tree;
Gates that fly open to the wind
And close again behind,
And fields that are a flowing sea
And make the cattle look like ships;
Straws glistening and stiff
Lying on air as on a shelf
And pond that leaps to leave itself;
And feathers too that rise and float,
Each feather changed into a bird,
And line-hung sheets that crack and strain;
Even the sun-greened coat,
That through so many winds has served,
The scarecrow struggles to put on again.

THE SCARECROW

by Walter de la Mare

All winter through I bow my head
   Beneath the driving rain;
The North Wind powders me with snow
   And blows me black again;
At midnight in a maze of stars
   I flame with glittering rime,
And stand, above the stubble, stiff
   As mail at morning-prime.
But when that child, called Spring, and all
   His host of children, come,
Scattering their buds and dew upon
   These acres of my home,
Some rapture in my rags awakes;
   I lift void eyes and scan
The skies for crows, those ravening foes,
   Of my strange master, Man.
I watch him striding lank behind
   His clashing team, and know
Soon will the wheat swish body high
   Where once lay sterile snow;
Soon shall I gaze across a sea
   of sun-begotten grain,
Which my unflinching watch hath sealed
   For harvest once again.

THE FOX

by C. Day Lewis

'Look, it's a fox!' – their two hearts spoke
Together. A fortunate day
That was when they saw him, a russet spark
Blown from the wood's long-smouldering dark
On to the woodside way.

There, on the ride, a dog fox paused.
Around him the shadows lay
Attentive suddenly, masked and poised;
And the watchers found themselves enclosed
In a circuit stronger than they.

He stood for some mystery only shared
By creatures of fire and clay.
They watched him stand with the masterless air
Of one who had the best right to be there –
Let others go or stay;

Then, with a flick of his long brush, sign
The moment and whisk it away.
Time flowed back, and the two walked on
Down the valley. They felt they were given a sign –
But of what, they could hardly say.

EMMONSAILS HEATH
IN WINTER

by John Clare

I love to see the old heaths withered brake
Mingle its crimpled leaves with furze and ling
While the old Heron from the lonely lake
Starts slow and flaps his melancholly wing
And oddling crow in idle motions swing
On the half rotten ash trees topmost twig
Beside whose trunk the gipsey makes his bed
Up flies the bouncing wood cock from the brig
Where a black quagmire quakes beneath the tread
The field fare chatters in the whistling thorn
And for the awe round field and closen rove
And coy bumbarrels twenty in a drove
Flit down the hedgrows in the frozen plain
And hang on little twigs and start again

SMALL BIRDS

by Peter Quennell

Small birds who sweep into a tree
– A storm of fluttering, stilled as suddenly,
Making the light slip round a shaken berry,
Swinging slim sunlight twigs uncertainly,
Are moved by ripples of light discontent
– Quick waves of anger, breaking through the tree
Into a foam of riot – voices high
And tart as a sloe-berry.

BIRDS' NESTS

by Edward Thomas

The summer nests uncovered by autumn wind,
Some torn, others dislodged, all dark,
Everyone sees them: low or high in tree,
Or hedge, or single bush, they hang like a mark.

Since there's no need of eyes to see them with
I cannot help a little shame
That I missed most, even at eye's level, till
The leaves blew off and made the seeing no game.

'Tis a light pang. I like to see the nests
Still in their places, now first known,
At home and by far roads. Boys never found them,
Whatever jays and squirrels may have done.

And most I like the winter nest deep-hid
That leaves and berries fell into:
Once a dormouse dined there on hazel nuts,
And grass and goose-grass seeds found soil and grew.

WINTER

by Robert Southey

A wrinkled crabbed man they picture thee,
Old Winter, with a ragged beard as grey
As the long moss upon the apple-tree;
Blue-lipt, an ice drop at thy sharp blue nose,
Close muffled up, and on thy dreary way
Plodding alone through sleet and drifting snows.
They should have drawn thee by the high-heapt hearth,
Old Winter! seated in thy great armed chair,
Watching the children at their Christmas mirth;
Or circled by them as thy lips declare
Some merry jest, or tale of murder dire,
Or troubled spirit that disturbs the night;
Pausing at times to rouse the smouldering fire,
Or taste the old October brown and bright.

HARD FROST

by Andrew Young

Frost called to water 'Halt!'
And crusted the moist snow with sparkling salt;
Brooks, their own bridges, stop,
And icicles in long stalactites drop,
And tench in water-holes
Lurk under gluey glass like fish in bowls.

In the hard-rutted lane
At every footstep breaks a brittle pane,
And tinkling trees ice-bound,
Changed into weeping willows, sweep the ground;
Dead boughs take root in ponds
And ferns on windows shoot their ghostly fronds.

But vainly the fierce frost
Interns poor fish, ranks trees in an armed host,
Hangs daggers from house-eaves
And on the windows ferny ambush weaves;
In the long war grown warmer
The sun will strike him dead and strip his armour.

WAITING FOR SNOW

by S.D.P. Clough

Row upon row
in their brown habits
The hills wait
for the coming of snow
like monks for Christ.

from WINTER

Anonymous (10th–11th century)

Wind sharp, hillside bleak, hard to win shelter;
    Ford is impassable, lake is frozen;
   A man may near stand on one stalk of grass.

    Wave upon wave roofs over land-edge;
Shouts loud against breast of peak and brae;
    Outside, a man may barely stand.

Lake-haunts cold, with the storm winds of winter;
    Withered the reeds, stalks all broken;
   Wind-gusts angry, stripping of woods.

Cold bed of fish in the gloom of ice;
    Stag lean, bearded reeds;
   Evening brief, slant of bent wood.

Snow falls, covers with white;
Warriors go not forth on foray;
Lakes cold, their tint without sunlight.

Translated from the Welsh by
Tony Conran

TAM SNOW

by Charles Causley

To Kaye Webb

Who in the bleak wood
Barefoot, ice-fingered,
Runs to and fro?
        Tam Snow.

Who, soft as a ghost,
Falls on our house to strike
Blow after blow?
        Tam Snow.

Who with a touch of the hand
Stills the world's sound
In its flow?
        Tam Snow.

Who holds to our side,
Though as friend or as foe
We never may know?
        Tam Snow.

Who hides in the hedge
After thaw, waits for more
Of his kind to show?
        Tam Snow.

Who is the guest
First we welcome, then
Long to see go?
        Tam Snow.

To a Snowflake

by Francis Thompson

What heart could have thought you? –
Past our devisal
(O filigree petal!)
Fashioned so purely,
Fragilely, surely,
From what Paradisal
Imagineless metal,
Too costly for cost?
Who hammered you, wrought you,
From argentine vapour? –
'God was my shaper.
Passing surmisal,
He hammered, He wrought me,
From curled silver vapour,
To lust of His mind: –
Thou could'st not have thought me!
So purely, so palely,
Tinily, surely,
Mightily, frailly,
Insculped and embossed,
With His hammer of wind,
And his graver of frost'.

THE REDBREAST

by Anthony Rye

The redbreast smoulders in the waste of snow:
His eye is large and bright, and to and fro
He draws and draws his slender threads of sound
Between the dark boughs and the freezing ground.

'Shaggy, and lean, and shrewd, with pointed ears'

by *William Cowper*
from *The Task* (Book V: The Winter Morning Walk)

Shaggy, and lean, and shrewd, with pointed ears
And tail cropp'd short, half lurcher and half cur –
His dog attends him. Close behind his heel
Now creeps he slow; and now, with many a frisk
Wide-scampering, snatches up the drifted snow
With ivory teeth, or ploughs it with his snout;
Then shakes his powder'd coat, and barks for joy.

'LO! FROM THE LIVID EAST OR PIERCING NORTH'

by James Thomson
from *The Seasons*

Lo! from the livid east or piercing north,
Thick clouds ascend, in whose capacious womb
A vapoury deluge lies, to snow congealed.
Heavy, they roll their fleecy world along,
And the sky saddens with th' impending storm.
Through the hushed air the whitening shower descends,
At first thin-wavering; till at last the flakes
Fall broad and wide and fast, dimming the day
With a continual flow. See! sudden hoared,
The woods beneath the stainless burden bow;
Black'ning, along the mazy stream it melts.
Earth's universal face, deep-hid and chill,
Is all one dazzling waste. The labourer-ox
Stands covered o'er with snow, and then demands
The fruit of all his toil.

. . . .

              The foodless wilds
Pour forth their brown inhabitants. The hare,
Though timorous of heart, and hard beset
By death in various forms, dark snares and dogs,
And more unpitying men, the garden seeks,
Urged on by fearless want. The bleating kind
Eye the bleak heavens, and next the glistening earth,
With looks of dumb despair; then sad, dispersed,
Dig for the withered herb though heaps of snow.

from **THE WHITE HARE**

by Lilian Bowes Lyon

At the field's edge,
In the snow-furred sedge,
Couches the white hare;
Her stronghold is there.

Brown as the seeding grass
In summer she was,
With a creamed belly soft as ermine;
Beautiful she was among vermin.
Silky young she had,
For her spring was glad;
. . . .
Thanks to her senses five
This charmer is alive:
Who cheated the loud pack,
Biting steel, poacher's sack;
Among the steep rocks
Outwitted the fanged fox.

And now winter has come;
Winds have made dumb
Water's crystal chime;
In a cloak of rime
Stands the stiff bracken;
Until the cold slacken
Beauty and terror kiss;
There is no armistice.
Low must the hare lie,
With great heart and round eye.

from THE DAFT-DAYS

by Robert Fergusson

Now mirk December's dowie face
Glours owr the rigs wi' sour grimace,
While, thro' his minimum of space,
      The bleer-eyed sun,
Wi' blinkin light and stealing pace,
      His race doth run.

From naked groves nae birdie sings,
To shepherd's pipe nae hillock rings,
The breeze nae od'rous flavour brings
      From Borean cave,
And dwyning nature droops her wings,
      Wi' visage grave.

Mankind but scanty pleasure glean
Frae snawy hill or barren plain,
Whan Winter, midst his nipping train,
      Wi' frozen spear,
Sends drift owr a' his bleak domain,
      And guides the weir.

In December

by Andrew Young

I watch the dung-cart stumble by
  Leading the harvest to the fields,
That from cow-byre and stall and sty
The farmstead in the winter yields.

Like shocks in a reaped field of rye
  The small black heaps of lively dung
Sprinkled in the grass-meadow lie
  Licking the air with smoky tongue.

This is Earth's food that man piles up
  And with his fork will thrust on her,
And Earth will lie and slowly sup
  With her moist mouth through half the year.

THE DARKLING THRUSH

by Thomas Hardy

I leant upon a coppice gate
　　When Frost was spectre-gray,
And Winter's dregs made desolate
　　The weakening eye of day.
The tangled bine-stems scored the sky
　　Like strings of broken lyres,
And all mankind that haunted nigh
　　Had sought their household fires.

The land's sharp features seemed to be
　　The Century's corpse outleant,
His crypt the cloudy canopy,
　　The wind his death-lament.
The ancient pulse of germ and birth
　　Was shrunken hard and dry,
And every spirit upon earth
　　Seemed fervourless as I.

At once a voice arose among
　　The bleak twigs overhead
In a full-hearted evensong
　　Of joy illimited;
An aged thrush, frail, gaunt, and small,
　　In blast-beruffled plume,
Had chosen thus to fling his soul
　　Upon the growing gloom.

So little cause for carolings
　　Of such ecstatic sound
Was written on terrestrial things
　　Afar or nigh around,
That I could think there trembled through
　　His happy good-night air
Some blessed Hope, whereof he knew
　　And I was unaware.

WINTER: EAST ANGLIA

by Edmund Blunden

In a frosty sunset
  So fiery red with cold
The footballers' onset
  Rings out glad and bold;
Then boys from daily tether
  With famous dogs at heel
In starlight meet together
  And to farther hedges steal;
Where the rats are pattering
  In and out the stacks,
Owls with hatred chattering
  Swoop at the terriers' backs.
And, frost forgot, the chase grows hot
  Till a rat's a foolish prize,
But the cornered weasel stands his ground,
Shrieks at the dogs and boys set round,
Shrieks as he knows they stand all round,
  And hard as winter dies.

THE PINES

by Andrew Young

The eye might fancy that those pines,
With snow-struck stems in pallid lines,
Were lit by the sunlight at noon,
Or shadow-broken gleam of the moon;
But snowflakes rustle down the air,
As though uncertain where to fall,
Filling the wood with a deep pall,
The wood that hastens darkness to hide all.

The hurricane of snow last night
Felled one; its roots, surprised by light,
Clutch at the air in wild embrace;
Peace like an echo fills the place
Save for the quiet labour of snow,
That falling flake on flake below
The torn limbs and the red wounds stanches,
And with a sheet the dead trunk blanches,
And lays white delicate wreaths among the branches.

BLACKBIRD

by Frank Prewett

Blackbird by pondered phrase
Talks in the eve of dusk,
In pale trembling sun when fails
The north which breathed all day,
And the lamb clouds melt to blue.
Blackbird from wintered elm
Deliberate and calm
Studies each phrase,
Each phrase for a full song.
Tongues of evening fire
Lick the elm top where he sings,
Where he quickens his phrase
And ruffles and arches and swells
And strides a pace on the black bough,
Clear fluting to me below
In the brief cold fiery dusk.

AT CANDLEMAS

by Charles Causley

'If Candlemas be fine and clear
There'll be two winters in that year';

But all the day the drumming sun
Brazened it out that spring had come,

And the tall elder on the scene
Unfolded the first leaves of green.

But when another morning came
With frost, as Candlemas with flame,

The sky was steel, there was no sun,
The elder leaves were dead and gone.

Out of a cold and crusted eye
The stiff pond stared up at the sky,

And on the scarcely breathing earth
A killing wind fell from the north;

But still within the elder tree
The strong sap rose, though none could see.

WINTER DUSK

by Herbert Read

Rain-filled ruts
reflect
an apple-green sky

Into black huts
a shawled woman
shoos her hissing geese

A cold wind
insinuates
the evening star

Bleak thorns
and wassail berries
hide the sweet thrush.

A Frosty Night

by Philip Callow

All night the constellations sang
there, in that perfect church, and rang
in the cold belfry of the night,
strewing their splintered light
over the bare sea and the humpbacked fields,
while the hammer of frost, that kills
a flower and leaves a feather
on the gatepost, swung from the weather.

All the lanes grooved round the hillsides
shrank; a brittle skin grew over the puddles;
a sharp wind sawed at the birches,
and the sleeping trunks and branches,
cracking their bark and their frozen flesh,
groaned out of a leafless peace,
and the catkins hung limp in the cruel air
where they had danced the day before.

In the clear morning a salt of frost,
flung down thickly by the moon's ghost,
lay on the roofs and the sloping grass
of the rough hills, sparkling like glass.
And like a warm beast in a shippen
the animal body of the sun
was struggling up, and with stiff knees
heaved itself out of the trees.

OUT IN THE DARK

by Edward Thomas

Out in the dark over the snow
The fallow fawns invisible go
With the fallow doe;
And the winds blow
Fast as the stars are slow.

Stealthily the dark haunts round
And, when the lamp goes, without sound
At a swifter bound
Than the swiftest hound,
Arrives, and all else is drowned;

And I and star and wind and deer,
Are in the dark together, – near,
Yet far, – and fear
Drums on my ear
In that sage company drear.

How weak and little is the light,
All the universe of sight,
Love and delight,
Before the might,
If you love it not, of night.

from **THE COLD EARTH SLEPT BELOW**

by Percy Bysshe Shelley

The cold earth slept below,
    Above the cold sky shone;
And all around, with a chilling sound,
From caves of ice and fields of snow,
The breath of night like death did flow
Beneath the sinking moon.

The wintry hedge was black,
    The green grass was not seen,
The birds did rest on the bare thorn's breast,
Whose roots, beside the pathway track,
Had bound their folds o'er many a crack
    Which the frost had made between.

THE YEAR'S ROUND

by Coventry Patmore

The crocus, while the days are dark,
Unfolds its saffron sheen;
At April's touch, the crudest bark
Discovers gems of green.

Then sleep the seasons, full of might;
While slowly swells the pod
And rounds the peach, and in the night
The mushroom bursts the sod.

The winter comes: the frozen rut
Is bound with silver bars;
The snow-drift heaps against the hut;
And night is pierced with stars.

Sonnet IV

by Hilaire Belloc

The Winter Moon has such a quiet car
That all the winter nights are dumb with rest.
She drives the gradual dark with drooping crest
And dreams go wandering from her drowsy star
Because the nights are silent do not wake
But there shall tremble through the general earth,
And over you, a quickening and a birth.
The Sun is near the hill-tops for your sake.

The latest born of all the days shall creep
To kiss the tender eyelids of the year;
And you shall wake, grown young with perfect sleep,
And smile at the new world and make it dear
   With living murmurs more than dreams are deep;
   Silence is dead, my dawn, the morning's here.

RED MIST

by M.E. Trenchard

The red mist in the Elm trees thickens,
As in the tree the spring sap quickens,
Am I the only one who sees,
Resurrection in the trees?

'THEREFORE ALL SEASONS SHALL BE SWEET TO THEE'

by Samuel Taylor Coleridge
from Frost at Midnight

Therefore all seasons shall be sweet to thee,
Whether the summer clothe the general earth
With greenness, or the redbreast sit and sing
Betwixt the tufts of snow on the bare branch
Of mossy apple-tree, while the nigh thatch
Smokes in the sun-thaw; whether the eave-drops fall
Heard only in the trances of the blast,
Or if the secret ministry of frost
Shall hang them up in silent icicles,
Quietly shining to the quiet Moon.

THAW

by Edward Thomas

Over the land freckled with snow half-thawed
The speculating rooks at their nests cawed
And saw from elm-tops, delicate as flower of grass,
What we below could not see, Winter pass.

'FOR ADORATION SEASONS CHANGE'

by Christopher Smart
from A Song to David
(Extracts)

For ADORATION seasons change,
And order, truth and beauty range,
Adjust, attract, and fill:
The grass the polyanthus cheques;
And polish'd porphyry reflects,
By the descending rill.

Rich almonds colour to the prime
For ADORATION; tendrils climb,
And fruit-trees pledge their gems;
And Ivis, with her gorgeous vest,
Builds for her eggs her cunning nest,
And bell-flowers bow their stems.

Now labour his reward receives,
For ADORATION counts his sheaves,
To peace, her bounteous prince;
The nectarine his strong tint imbibes,
And apples of ten thousand tribes,
And quick peculiar quince.

The laurels with the winter strive;
The crocus burnishes alive
Upon the snow-clad earth:
For ADORATION myrtles stay
To keep the garden from dismay,
And bless the sight from dearth.

The pheasant shows his pompous neck;
And ermine, jealous of a speck,
With fear eludes offence:
The sable with his glossy pride,
For ADORATION is descried,
Where frosts the wave condense.

The cheerful holly, pensive yew,
And holy thorn, their trim renew;
The squirrel hoards his nuts:
All creatures batten o'er their stores,
And careful nature all her doors
For ADORATION shuts.

INDEX OF POETS

INDEX OF TITLES

261

INDEX OF FIRST LINES

Italics are used for extracts